CHOLESTEROL CURE MADE EASY

SYLVAN R. LEWIS, M.D.

WINGS BOOKS
New York • Avenel, New Jersey

This 1993 edition is published by Wings Books,
distributed by Outlet Book Company, Inc., a Random House Company,
40 Engelhard Avenue, Avenel, New Jersey 07001,
by arrangement with Fell Publishers, Inc.

Random House
New York • Toronto • London • Sydney • Auckland

Printed and bound in the United States of America

Library of Congress Cataloging-in-Publication Data

Lewis, Sylvan R.
    Cholesterol cure made easy / Sylvan R. Lewis.
        p.   cm.
    Originally published under title: Cholesterol C.U.R.E. made easy;
Hollywood, Fla.: Fell Publishers, 1989.
    ISBN 0-517-08904-1
    1. Low-cholesterol diet.   I. Title.
RM237.75.L49   1992
616. 1'320654—dc20   92-34868
                                                          CIP

10 9 8 7 6 5 4 3 2 1

TABLE OF CONTENTS

INTRODUCTION

Ask yourself the following questions:

* Have you ever had a blood cholesterol reading of 220 or above?
* Do you have high blood pressure?
* Do you smoke cigarettes?
* Are you overweight? *very* overweight? obese?
* Do you exercise regularly? occasionally? at all?
* Does your family have a history of heart disease, high blood pressure, heart attack, or stroke?
* Do you understand how your current lifestyle can play a role in the development of chronic illness—including heart disease? *Are you doing anything about this?*

Cardiovascular disease is the leading cause of death in this country. There are a number of known contributing factors to cardiovascular disease (CVD), including:

* elevated blood cholesterol levels (hyperlipidemia)
* high blood pressure (hypertension)
* cigarette smoking
* obesity (significant overweight)
* lack of exercise
* poorly controlled stress
* family history of heart disease

Of these, only one cannot be altered. But, you *can* control the rest of them by:

* quitting smoking
* altering your diet
* shedding excess weight
* exercising regularly
* controlling daily stress

If you are not a cigarette smoker, the most important risk factor for you to control is your *blood cholesterol level*. By lowering your elevated cholesterol, you can significantly reduce your chances of suffering a heart attack or stroke, and you can significantly reduce the atherosclerotic build-up clogging your arteries. And, you can accomplish these health-saving steps simply by altering your current lifestyle—including your diet.

Your diet serves as the cornerstone in the foundation of your well-being. Change your diet to better support your overall health, and you will improve your body—inside and out. The food you eat makes a major impact on your physical self—your looks and build, state of health, and risk for heart disease and other chronic ills.

Once you have a basic understanding of how your diet influences your health, you can then make the necessary changes in the foods you choose to eat. To encourage you to make these changes, the U.S. Surgeon General has issued a special report on nutrition and health. The dietary recommendations provided in this landmark report include:

* Reduce consumption of fat (especially saturated fat) and cholesterol
* Achieve and maintain a desirable body weight
* Increase consumption of complex carbohydrates and fiber
* Reduce the intake of sodium
* Take alcohol only in moderation, if at all

Each of these recommendations can help to reduce your risk for heart attack and stroke. The Surgeon General's suggestions can help you to prevent or reverse the process of atherosclerosis. The Surgeon General's dietary guidelines can save your life!

If you are willing to make some changes in your eating habits and lifestyle patterns, this book can help you lower your cholesterol and prevent cardiovascular disease—safely, easily, and naturally. There is no need to purchase expensive and risky nutritional supplements. And, unless your doctor has prescribed them, there is no need to turn to costly drugs and suffer from the associated side effects. You can eat your way toward a healthy heart, using the information provided in this book, by making some simple changes in the foods you choose. You can cure your cholesterol woes—naturally!

Read on to discover:

* How dietary cholesterol and fats increase blood cholesterol, and which foods to minimize or avoid.
* What types of fats reduce blood cholesterol, and where to find them.

* How certain minerals can detract from heart
    health (i.e. sodium) while others enhance it (i.e.
    calcium, magnesium, potassium).
* How fiber influences blood cholesterol, and the
    best food sources for this.
* The ultimate cholesterol cure – safe weight loss,
    with proper diet and regular exercise.

IMPORTANT NOTE: *See your physician before undertaking this or any other diet!*

ACKNOWLEDGEMENT: Professional assistance was provided by Virginia Aronson, R.D., M.S., a registered dietitian and nutrition writer. Author of more than a dozen books, Ms. Aronson's most recent publication is *The I Don't Eat (But I Can't Lose) Weight Loss Program* (Rawson/Macmillan, 1989).

HOW TO USE THIS BOOK

First, answer the following question: Are you ready, willing, and able to change your diet to improve your health? If not, you may want to ask yourself why you cannot make the effort to improve the quality of your life. Because until you do so, dietary change and optimal health may continue to elude you.

If you answered a firm "yes," or even if you are not quite sure, the information and diet guidance provided in this book *can* assist you in changing your diet to reduce your cholesterol and improve your health.

Ready? Good! Read through the next 21 pages to learn the nutritional facts and identify which foods to eat or avoid. Use the sample menus in Chapter 4 to get yourself started on a low-cholesterol, low-sodium, low-calorie eating plan. You'll soon see how simple (and tasty!) it is to eat *healthfully*. Whenever you dine out, use the list of DINING OUT DO'S AND DON'TS to help you select foods *wisely*. The FOOD VALUE LIST can assist you further in choosing foods *carefully*, while the MENU PLANNING LISTS can help you to plan daily menus, *easily*.

You have everything at your fingertips for beginning a new way of eating. If you choose to, if you are ready and willing, this book can enable you to eat healthfully and wisely, carefully yet easily. You *can* lower your cholesterol naturally. The choice is yours!

CHOLESTEROL AND YOUR HEALTH

The primary recommendation of the U.S. Surgeon General's nutrition report is to reduce the amount of fat and *cholesterol* in our diets. Why? How?

Why Worry

Cholesterol is a waxy, fat-like substance that is manufactured in the liver and provided by dietary intake. The level of cholesterol in your bloodstream is determined by the amount produced by your body and by the composition of your diet. The intake of certain fats, called "*saturated* fats," stimulates cholesterol production, and consumption of *cholesterol*-rich foods contributes to blood levels. The intake of other fats, called "*polyunsaturated* fats," "*monounsaturated* fats," and "*omega-3 fatty acids*," help to reduce blood cholesterol. And, certain *fibers* can lower cholesterol levels as well.

Cholesterol plays an important role in a variety of the body's functions, including the production of sex hormones and the bile necessary for proper digestion. Cholesterol is actually a constituent of every cell in the body. However, *too much* cholesterol in the body is harmful.

The amount of cholesterol in the bloodstream is reflective of the degree of "atherosclerosis" in the body; that is, the progress of the disease responsible for heart attacks, circulatory disorders, and strokes. Atherosclerosis is a form of arteriosclerosis, or hardening of the arteries, a process by which fatty materials (including cholesterol) are deposited in the linings of the arteries. The deposits form rough "plaques," gradually building up to narrow arterial passages. If an artery becomes completely blocked, blood is unable to flow through, cutting off the delivery of essential oxygen and nutrients to the organ it supplies.

If the artery that supplies the heart tissue (coronary artery) is blocked, the result is "angina" (chest pains warning of inadequate oxygen supply to the heart) and possibly heart attack ("coronary" or myocardial infarction). If the artery that supplies the extremities is blocked, circulatory disorders and claudication can result. And, if the arterial supply to the brain is blocked, the result is episodes of dizziness and blurred vision, possibly followed by stroke. Thus, cholesterol build-up contributes to atherosclerosis, which causes America's number one killer: cardiovascular disease.

How to Measure Cholesterol

Fortunately, you can take preventive steps against the threat of cardiovascular disease. By controlling the degree of cholesterol build-up in your bloodstream, you can minimize the amount of plaque in your arteries and reduce your risk for heart attack and stroke. New studies indicate that you can even *reverse* cholesterol build-up to diminish the plaque which has already formed in your arterial passage ways.

The first step to take is to have your physician order a simple laboratory test to determine your "blood lipid profile." The test results will reveal the total amount of cholesterol and other fats (lipids) in your bloodstream. Standards of interpretation vary from physician to physician, but most agree that total blood cholesterol over 220 is undesirably high. (The values for populations where cardiovascular disease is rare can range as low as 130-140!) The profile will also show the levels of "LDL" and "HDL" forms of blood fats, an important test result to interpret.

Cholesterol is transported in the blood by protein carriers of different sizes known as "lipoproteins." The lightest or "low density lipoproteins" (LDL) carry most of the cholesterol. High levels of LDL in the blood are associated with increased risk for cardiovascular disease. The heavier, high density lipoproteins (HDL) assist in the removal of cholesterol from body tissues. Thus, a high level of HDLs is indicative of a low risk for heart attack and stroke. The best test results, therefore, will reveal a total cholesterol of 200 or below, with a high ratio of HDLs and a low degree of LDLs. Your physician can help you to interpret your blood lipid profile properly.

What to Do

If test results reveal an elevated blood cholesterol with an undesirable ratio of HDL:LDL, it is time to make some dietary changes. Your physician may prescribe a lipid-lowering drug, but most doctors prefer to begin with a diet program in the hopes that medication will prove unnecessary. If test results reveal a "normal" blood lipid profile, you may choose to improve your eating habits anyway—to make sure your cardiovascular system remains strong and healthy.

The dietary prescription for a healthy heart is referred to as the "Prudent Diet." This is a well-balanced, nutritious diet plan that is low in cholesterol and saturated fat, low in sodium, and calorically controlled to allow for the attainment and maintenance of a healthy body weight. This book provides you with the information and guidance needed to adopt and adhere to a Prudent Diet—for life!

Cholesterol in Foods

Perhaps the clearest step to take toward eating prudently is to *reduce dietary cholesterol*. The Prudent Diet minimizes highcholesterol foods, notably egg yolks, organ meats, fatty meats, such as bacon and burgers, butter, cream, and whole milk products. The suggested daily *maximum* cholesterol intake is 300 mg. A single egg yolk contains some 280 mg., while an egg white is cholesterol-free. So, eggs are limited to one to two yolks per week. Organ meats (liver, kidney, sweetbreads) should be eaten no more than once a month. Other high-cholesterol foods (see list below) can be avoided entirely, or eaten in limited amounts on occasion, if desired. The choice is yours.

High Cholesterol Foods List

bacon	half & half
burgers	hot dogs
butter	ice cream
caviar	lard
cheese (unless low-fat)	milk, whole
cold cuts	organ meats (kidney, liver)
cream	salt pork
cream cheese	sausages
egg yolk	sour cream
eggnog	whipped cream
fatty meat (choice, marbled, and prime cuts; ground meats; spareribs)	

FATS AND YOUR HEALTH

The average American diet contains more than 40 percent of the total caloric intake as fat. This is an *unhealthy*, excessive amount. The Prudent Diet limits fat intake to 30 to 35 percent, and emphasizes foods rich in *healthful* fats.

Types of Fats

Lipid is the general scientific term for fats. The majority of the lipids in your body and your diet are triglycerides, which in foods are mostly *saturated* or *unsaturated* in form. And lipids are not all bad, despite the negative press they have been receiving.

In your body, fat is the storage form of energy required for muscular work. Fat also cushions vital organs and insulates the body to provide internal temperature control.

Fat is a dietary essential because it transports certain vitamins (the "fat-soluble" vitamins A, D, E, and K), and the fatty acid ("linoleic" acid) important for growth and health. Fat also provides flavor and satiety, increasing eating enjoyment.

It would be undesirable – and practically impossible – to eliminate all fat from the diet. The key to a Prudent Diet is to *moderate* total fat intake and to emphasize the more healthful types of fat.

Saturated fats are usually hard at room temperature and are found mainly in animal foods, such as meats, whole milk, butter, cream, and lard. Several vegetable oils are highly saturated: coconut and palm oil. And, when vegetable oils are "hydrogenated," that is, processed with a solid form, they become more saturated. Thus, foods prepared with coconut, palm, and/or hydrogenated vegetable oils tend to be high in saturated fats. Typical examples included commercial baked goods, chips, non-dairy creamers, stick margarines, shortening, and foods fried in the saturated oils. Since products made with saturated fats tend to have a long shelf-life, many processed foods are highly saturated. Unfortunately, *saturated fats contribute to an elevated blood cholesterol level.*

Unsaturated fats tend to be liquid at room temperatures, while the "polyunsaturated" fats are abundant in most vegetable oils, including:

* safflower oil
* sunflower oil
* cottonseed oil
* corn oil
* sesame oil
* soybean oil

Diets low in total fat with an emphasis on polyunsaturated fats help to reduce blood cholesterol levels. Thus, the Prudent Diet minimizes intake of choices from the HIGH SAT-FATS FOODS LIST below, partially substituting the polyunsaturated vegetable oils listed above.

High Sat-Fats Foods List

bacon
biscuits
burgers
butter
cakes
cheese (unless low-fat)
chips
chocolate, cocoa butter
coconut
coconut butter
cold cuts
cookies
cream
creamers, non-dairy
cream cheese
croissants
Danish
doughnuts
fatty meats (choice, marbled, prime cuts; ground meats; spareribs)

french fries
granolas, commercial
gravies
half & half
hot dogs
hydrogenated vegetable oils
ice cream
lard
margarine, stick
milk, whole
palm oil
pastries
pies
salt pork
sausages
shortening
sour cream
whipped cream
fried foods (chicken, fish, potatoes, potato skins, vegetables)

DIET CURES: THE UN-FATS

Until recently, the medical community was unaware of the fact that "monounsaturated" fats can help lower blood cholesterol. Due to this relatively new discovery, physicians and nutritionists now recommend a Prudent Diet which includes foods rich in these unsaturated fats.

Another recent diet discovery is the important role of "omega-3 fatty acids" in human health. This type of unsaturated fat contributes to a reduced risk of cardiovascular disease, as diets rich in omega-3's help to lower blood cholesterol levels, reduce blood pressure and clotting, and inhibit atherosclerosis. The omega-3 fatty acids are abundant in cold water fish, and are found in all marine life, including shellfish.

By reducing total fat intake to 30 to 35 percent, and *substituting monounsaturated fats and food rich in omega-3 fatty acids* for saturated fats, you can lower your cholesterol level significantly. Select foods from the two lists that follow, the MONO-FAT FOODS LIST and the OMEGA-3 FOODS LIST, to partially replace the saturated fats in your diet. For example, substitute a broiled fish dinner for red meats several times a week. Stir-fry vegetables in peanut oil, and use olive oil in tomato sauce and other dishes. Snack on moderate amounts of cashews and peanuts, and indulge more often on shellfish, like crab or shrimp. Your heart, if not your wallet, can afford it!

Mono-Fat Foods List

almonds	olive oil
avocados	peanut oil
cashews	peanuts
filberts (hazelnuts)	pecans
olives	seafood

Omega-3 Foods List
Richest Sources

anchovies	mackerel
bluefish	salmon
halibut	trout, lake
herring	tuna

Also Good Sources

clams	mussels
cod	oysters
crab	scallops
flounder	shrimp
haddock	swordfish
lobster	and other cold water fish

MINERALS TO MONITOR

Minerals are naturally occurring elements, and there are seventeen essential to human health. These "essential" minerals work together to form healthy body tissues and regulate proper body function. Several minerals play important roles in cardiovascular function and health.

Calcium is essential for bone formation and strength, and assists in nerve transmission, muscle contraction, and heartbeat. Inadequate dietary calcium has been associated with high blood pressure. Foods rich in calcium (but low in fat) include:

* skim and lowfat milk, yogurt, cheeses

* salmon and sardines (with bones)
* green leafy vegetables (eg. broccoli and
    bok choy)
* tofu

Magnesium is essential for nerve conduction, muscle relaxation, and body energy. Deficiencies can occur with alcoholism, diuretic ("water pill") use, and inadequate dietary intake. A diet deficient in this mineral may lead to high blood pressure and heart failure. Foods rich in magnesium include:

* almonds, filberts, peanuts
* dried beans and peas
* whole grains, including oats
* seafoods

Potassium is critical for proper heartbeat. Gradual potassium depletion can occur with heavy sweating, diarrhea, and diuretic use. Diets deficient in this essential mineral have been associated with high blood pressure. Potassium-rich foods include:

* citrus fruits and juices
* bananas, strawberries, dried fruits
* tomatoes, broccoli, brussel sprouts, carrots,
    spinach
* corn, potatoes, sweet potatoes
* skim and lowfat milk

Sodium and Your Health

Sodium is actually an essential mineral, despite the bad things said about this nutrient. Sodium plays an important role in the body's regulation of fluids, and is essential for proper nerve transmission and muscle contraction. A depletion of this mineral can occur with dehydration due to illness, diuretic use, or heavy sweating. However, sodium is so ample in the typical diet that is easy to obtain adequate amounts. In fact, most Americans consume *far too much sodium*. And for those individuals who are "sodium sensitive," excessive dietary sodium causes high blood pressure.

Since it is not yet possible to detect who is "sodium sensitive," the medical community (and the U.S. Surgeon General) suggest that *everyone* moderate sodium intake. For those with hypertension, adherence to a low-sodium diet can dramatically lower high blood pressure. The simplest way to reduce the sodium in your diet is by not using the salt shaker (salt is "sodium chloride," containing 40 percent sodium or 2,000 mg. per teaspoon). And, by avoiding or minimizing your intake from the HIGH SODIUM FOODS LIST that follows, you can reduce your sodium intake to a prudent, healthful level.

High Sodium Foods List

bacon	ham
biscuits	lox
bouillon	packaged dinners, mixes
canned fish	pastrami
canned meats	pickles
catsup	pretzels
caviar	relishes
chips	sauerkraut
chipped beef	sausages
cold cuts	smoked fish
corned beef	smoked meats
crackers (unless unsalted)	soups
dips	soysauce
dried meats	stews
fast foods	tomato juice
frozen dinners	vegetable juice cocktail

salts: celery, garlic, onion, sea, seasoned, table, monosodium glutamate (MSG)

seasonings: cooking wines, meat extracts, meat tenderizers and marinades

medications: antacids, antibiotics, buffered headache remedies, cough medicines, laxatives, sedatives, sodium bicarbonate (baking soda), plus certain mouthwashes

FIBER FACTS

Fiber has been recognized for a number of years as a food element important for proper digestive processes. Since fiber is largely indigestible, fibrous foods pass rapidly through the digestive tract, assisting in efficient elimination and preventing constipation, hemorrhoids, and other bowel disorders.

There are several types of fiber, each with different physical properties and roles in human health. The "insoluble" fibers found in wheat bran, whole wheat products, fruits and vegetables speed digestion. Recent research has uncovered an essential function of the "soluble" fibers found in oat bran, dried beans, and peas. This type of fiber interferes with the absorption of fats and cholesterol, and diets rich in soluble fiber can help to lower blood lipids.

Most Americans consume inadequate amounts of dietary fiber. The Prudent Diet includes ample servings of foods rich in "complex carbohydrates" (starches) and fiber, emphasizing the dietary sources of soluble fibers:

* oat bran and whole oats (including oatmeal)
* oat bran cereals, breads, muffins
* whole oat cereals, breads, muffins
* kidney beans, navy beans, black beans, white beans
* black-eyed peas, split peas, chickpeas
* lentils, soybeans, tofu

By including generous servings of the foods containing soluble fibers listed above, while following a Prudent Diet containing plenty of low-calorie carbohydrate-rich and fibrous foods from the HIGH FIBER FOODS LIST below, you can reduce your blood cholesterol levels and enjoy a surprising side benefit: gradual weight loss!

High Fiber Foods List

bran, oat bran	nuts bran
cereals	peanut butter
breads, whole grain	popcorn
cereals, whole grain	rice, brown
crackers, whole grain	rice, wild
fig cookies	wheat germ

fruit — especially apples, berries, grapes, peaches, plums, and dried fruit

vegetables — especially broccoli, brussel sprouts, cabbage, carrots, cauliflower, corn, dried beans and peas, greens, and potatoes (with the skin)

THE ULTIMATE DIET CURE

Being overweight is not only unattractive, it is hazardous to your health! Excess poundage can contribute to the development of:

* respiratory problems
* diabetes
* gallbladder disorders
* difficulties with fertility and pregnancy
* chronic joint pain and arthritis
* certain types of cancer including breast cancer
* CARDIOVASCULAR DISEASE

Overweight individuals are at increased risk for:
* HIGH BLOOD PRESSURE
* STROKE
* CORONARY HEART DISEASE
* ELEVATED BLOOD CHOLESTEROL

Weight reduction has been shown to reduce high blood pressure and high blood cholesterol levels, improving blood lipid profiles by reducing both total cholesterol and LDL levels. If you are very overweight (more than 50 pounds over your DESIRED WEIGHT, as given in the table in the APPENDIX), gradual weight loss will probably bring down your cholesterol level. Even if you only have 10, 15 or 20 pounds to lose, a well-balanced weight reduction program can help to lower your blood cholesterol significantly. And if your blood pressure is above normal, weight loss may correct this problem as well. Attaining and maintaining a healthy weight can be the ultimate boon to your cardiovascular system— and to your overall health.

Calories and Your Health

More than one-quarter of the adults living in this country today are overweight. An increasing number of children and teenagers are also developing weight problems. Emotionally and physically, excess weight is a heavy burden to bear—at any age. Overweight people are often tired and become easily fatigued. They are more susceptible to accidents and infections, and suffer more from ill health. And, in an image-conscious society which values thinness and fitness as cultural virtues, the psychological stress of looking "unacceptable" can cause depression and emotional problems.

Being overweight can shorten your lifespan, in addition to making your day-to-day life less healthful and more difficult. Excess poundage is a physical, emotional, and social burden. Yet, it is a problem that *you can cure*—if you really want to.

Do you need to lose some weight? Do you *want* to lose that excess poundage? Ask yourself the following question: "What is my fat doing for me?" Be honest with yourself:

* Do you use your fat to keep people from getting close?
* Do you use your weight problem to avoid personal relationships?
* Do you use your fat to avoid sexual relationships?
* Do you overeat to try to fill an emotional emptiness?
* Do you worry that your social life would remain unsatisfying after you lost weight?
* Are you unwilling to make the commitment and the effort required to lose weight?
* Is it just plain *easier* to stay fat?

Face it. Your most important physical traits are your looks and your health. And, you can neither look nor feel your best if you are too fat. If you're fat, you probably aren't fit. And if you're overweight, you're not in optimal health. So what's it going to be, fat or fit, status quo or *a whole new you*?

Diet Made Easy

If you are overweight, it probably took many months, even years, for your body to have gotten into the shape that it is in now. So, you need to accept the fact that it will take time for you to reverse the process, to get into good physical shape, to become fit and healthy. By committing yourself to a well-balanced weight loss plan, you will be able to:

* lose the weight you need to lose – gradually, safely, permanently
* enjoy a wide variety of foods – in moderate amounts
* lower high blood pressure
* reduce elevated blood cholesterol
* increase your fitness level
* increase both the length of your life and the degree of physical and emotional health with which you live it.

A well-balanced diet which supplies your body with the proper amounts of nutrients does not have to be like a maze you are lost in, nor like a prison sentence you are forced to suffer through. This book provides you with the U.S. Department of Agriculture's caloric values so that you can build a diet based on a wide variety of foods. Also included are A MONTH OF MENUS with nutritious and delicious low-calorie meals and snack ideas (that are low in cholesterol and sodium as well).

You can use the DESIRED WEIGHTS table in the APPENDIX as a guide in determining a healthy weight goal to work toward. The average number of calories required to maintain your desired weight is given in the tables. Note that adjustments are made for age. You can, however, overcome the age-related decline in caloric requirements by increasing your physical activity level.

The Magic Key: Exercise

Weight control is based on a simple caloric equation: take in *more* calories than you use up in day-to-day activity and you gain weight; take in *less* calories than your body is using and you'll lose weight. However, a low-calorie diet *without regular exercise* will gradually lose effectiveness as the body adapts to the reduced caloric intake. This is one of the major reasons why over 90 percent of all dieters fail. They grow discouraged OR depressed with slowed success *because they cut calories without adding exercise*. Exercise is *the* key to long-term success with weight loss!

This does not mean you need to transform yourself into a marathon runner or professional athlete overnight. In order to enhance the weight loss process, you need only begin a regular program of "aerobic" exercise such as walking, jogging, bicycling, or swimming. By exercising 20-30 minutes 5-6 times a week, you will burn off extra calories, tone your muscles, and rev up your body's metabolism to further aid weight loss efforts. Plus, regular exercise will help reduce your blood pressure, and can improve your blood lipid profile by lowering total cholesterol and boosting the HDLs to a healthy ratio. Aerobic exercise strengthens the cardiovascular system while speeding weight loss — a double plus!

Choose from the following physical activities to burn calories while getting fit. Aerobic exercises are indicated by an asterisk (*).

Slow and Easy

In order to be successful in your weight loss efforts, it is essential for you to be patient. Begin your new low-cholesterol, low-sodium, low-calorie diet *slowly and carefully*. Use the sample menus in Chapter 4 to ease your palate and your psyche into the healthy way of eating. Begin on your exercise program in this same manner; that is, *slowly and carefully*. If you overdo with physical activity, you will probably become stiff, sore, and turned off to exercise. So start with a daily walk around the block, and advance *gradually* from there. Remember, it has taken some time for your body to get into its current shape, so it will take some time for you to diet and exercise yourself into the fit new you. Go for it!

NOTE: Crash diets appear on a regular basis in the popular press and on TV, luring the overweight with promises for "easy" weight loss and "overnight" fat loss. Americans spend millions of dollars every year on fad diet plans and potions, "magical" food supplements and pills. Yet, the only thing lost is the money wasted on these weight loss rip-offs! *Crash diets do not work*, and many are dangerous. Unbalanced diet plans can cause nutritional deficiencies and ill health. Nutrient supplements can prove toxic in large doses. And *very* low-calorie diets (1,000 calories per day or less) are not only unhealthy, but *slow down the body's metabolism so that weight loss is halted*. So, don't be fooled into trying a crash diet. Your patience will pay off with a fit 'n trim new you!

ENERGY EXPENDITURE BY A 150 POUND PERSON IN VARIOUS ACTIVITIES**

Activity Energy Cost:	Calories per Hour
Rest and Light Activity	50-200
Lying down or sleeping	80
Sitting	100
Driving an automobile	120
Standing	140
Domestic work	180
Moderate Activity	200-350
* Bicycling (5½ mph)	210
* Walking (2½ mph)	210
Gardening	220
Gymnastics	220
Canoeing (2½ mph)	230
Golf	250
* Lawn mowing (power mower)	250
Bowling	270
Lawn mowing (hand mower)	270

Fencing 300
Rowboating (2½ mph) 300
* Walking (3-3/4 mph) 300
Badminton 300
Horseback riding (trotting) 350
* Square dancing 350
Volleyball 350
* Roller skating 350

Vigorous Activity . . . . .over 350
Table tennis 360
Ditch digging (hand shovel) 400
* Ice skating (10 mph) 400
* Skiing, cross country 400
Wood chopping or sawing 400
* Swimming — side stroke 400
competitive 520
Tennis 420
* Jogging — 11.5 min/mile 455
9.0 min/mile 645
8.0 min/mile 715
Basketball 460
Water skiing 480
* Hill climbing (100 ft. per hour) 490
Skiing, downhill (10 mph) 600
Squash and handball 600
* Cycling (13 mph) 660
Racquetball 715
* Running — 7.0 min/mile 800
6.0 min/mile 900
* Scull rowing, competitive 840

**Adapted from: U.S. Government Printing Office brochure #040-000-0037-1 ("Exercise and Weight Control"). Where available, actual measured values have been used, for other values a "best guess" was made.

A MONTH OF MENUS

Here are 30 well-balanced meals low in cholesterol, sodium, and calories. Special foods are included to help reduce your cholesterol levels and body weight.

DAY ONE

BREAKFAST   1/2 cup orange juice
1 cup oatmeal with
   1 Tbsp raisins and
   1/2 cup skim or lowfat milk
herbal tea or coffee

LUNCH   3-4 oz canned salmon on a bed of lettuce
   with sliced cucumbers and tomato
1/4-1/2 cup lowfat yogurt or cottage cheese
3-4 whole rye crackers
fresh peach
iced tea or club soda

DINNER   1 cup whole wheat spaghetti with
   1/2 cup tomato sauce (made with
    olive oil) and
   1 tsp Parmesan cheese
1/2 cup steamed Italian-cut beans
tossed green salad with
   lowfat Italian dressing
4 oz dry red wine or club soda with lime

SNACK   1 cup skim or lowfat milk
1-2 graham crackers

DAY TWO

BREAKFAST   1/2 med grapefruit
1-2 sm oat bran muffins
1 cup skim or lowfat milk
herbal tea or coffee

LUNCH   Spinach salad:
fresh spinach leaves, fresh mushroom
slices, grated hard-cooked egg white, 2
anchovies—topped with olive
oil-vinegar-lemon dressing
1 sm whole-wheat pita pocket
1 med apple
iced tea or club soda

DINNER   chicken stir-fry:
1-2 cups mixed vegetables (celery, bell
peppers, carrots, zucchini, water
chestnuts, peapods, mushrooms)
3 oz chicken, cut in thin strips,
stir fried in
1-2 tsp peanut oil
1 cup brown rice
1/2 cup pineapple chunks
tea

SNACK   1 cup lowfat yogurt (vanilla, coffee, or
lemon-flavored)

DAY THREE

BREAKFAST 1/2 cup apple juice
1 cup bran cereal with
   1/2 sm banana, sliced, and
   1/2 cup skim or lowfat milk
herbal tea or coffee

LUNCH peanut butter sandwich:
   2 sl whole wheat bread with
   1-2 tsp peanut butter and
   1-2 tsp all-fruit strawberry preserve
1 cup skim or lowfat milk
1 sm box (1-1/2 oz) raisins

DINNER oysters on the half shell (1 cup or 10-15)
   with fresh horseradish
tossed salad with
   lowfat avocado dressing
1/2 cup steamed green beans with
   1 tsp slivered almonds
1 sm slice angelfood cake with
   1/4 cup fresh strawberries
iced tea or club soda

SNACK 1/4 cup hummus with
   vegetable sticks (celery, carrots, bell
      peppers, etc.)

DAY FOUR

BREAKFAST 1/2 cup pineapple juice
1 cup hot oat bran cereal with
   1 Tbsp raisins and
   1/2 cup skim or lowfat milk
herbal tea or coffee

LUNCH tuna fish sandwich:
   3-1/2 oz canned tuna mixed with
      1-2 Tbsp lowfat yogurt
      chopped celery
      green pepper
      onion, garnished with
      lettuce leaves on
   2 sl pumpernickel bread
1 cup skim or lowfat milk
1 med pear

DINNER 3 oz lean veal roast
1/2 lg sweet potato, baked and mashed
1/2 cup wild rice
1 cup steamed broccoli with lemon
1/4 cup fresh fruit sorbet
iced tea or club soda

SNACK 2-3 cups popcorn

DAY FIVE

BREAKFAST   1/2 sm melon filled with
  1/2 cup lowfat cottage cheese and
  10-12 grapes, seedless
1 sl oatmeal bread, toasted with
  1 tsp marmalade or all-fruit preserve
herbal tea or coffee

LUNCH   1 cup meatless chili with
  1 tsp grated Parmesan cheese
3-4 whole wheat crackers
fresh tangerine
iced tea or club soda

DINNER   3-4 oz broiled swordfish with lemon
1 med red potato, baked
1 cup steamed brussel sprouts
tossed salad with
  lowfat French dressing
1 cup skim or lowfat milk

SNACK   1 cup lowfat yogurt with
  1/2 cup blueberries

DAY SIX

BREAKFAST 1/2 cup orange juice
1 cup oat bran flakes with
    1/2 sm banana, sliced, and
    1/2 cup skim or lowfat milk
herbal tea or coffee

LUNCH health salad:
    Romaine lettuce with
    sliced cucumber, red pepper,
      mushrooms, and
    1/2 cup bean sprouts, garnish with
    chickpeas, kidney beans, and
      (3 Tbsp) slivered almonds topped
      with olive oil-vinegar-lemon dressing
1-2 whole wheat breadsticks
2 pineapple rings
iced tea or club soda

DINNER 3 oz roasted turkey breast
1/2 cup barley stuffing (made without
    egg yolk or butter)
1 cup steamed baby carrots with fresh mint
    garnish
1/2 cup baby sweet peas
baked apple with honey and raisins
iced tea or club soda

SNACK 1 cup skim or lowfat milk
1-2 fig cookies

DAY SEVEN

BREAKFAST 1/2 med grapefruit
1 egg, poached, on
   1 sl oatmeal toast
1 cup skim or lowfat milk
herbal tea or coffee

LUNCH bagel broiler:
   1 whole wheat or rye bagel, broiled with
   1-1/2 oz lowfat cheese and
   sliced tomato
1 cup fruit salad
iced tea or club soda

DINNER baked vegetable casserole:
   1 cup chopped spinach and/or broccoli
     mixed with
      1/2 cup cooked red kidney beans
      1/2 cup cooked brown rice, and
      sauteed onions
      garlic
      mushrooms; top with
   1 oz part-skim mozzarella cheese, in
     strips
tossed salad with
   lowfat avocado dressing
nectarine
iced tea or club soda

SNACK 1 light beer or 3 oz dry white wine
1 oz cashews or peanuts

DAY EIGHT

BREAKFAST 1/2 cup orange juice
1 cup oatmeal with
   1 Tbsp chopped dates and
   1/2 cup skim or lowfat milk
herbal tea or coffee

LUNCH salad nicoise:
   Romaine lettuce tossed with
      3-1/2 oz canned tuna,
      1/2 cup white beans,
      wedges of tomato, and
      1 sm boiled potato, cut in wedges
        topped with
      lowfat Italian dressing
3-4 whole rye crackers
fresh peach
iced tea or club soda

DINNER 1 cup whole grain pasta with
   1/2 cup tomato sauce (made with
      olive oil) and
   1 tsp grated Parmesan cheese
1 sm whole wheat roll
1 cup steamed cauliflower with lemon
1 cup skim or lowfat milk

SNACK 1 cup lowfat yogurt with
1/2 cup blueberries

DAY NINE

BREAKFAST   1/2 med grapefruit
1-2 sm oat bran muffins
1 cup skim or lowfat milk
herbal tea or coffee

LUNCH   Greek salad:
    iceberg lettuce with
        sliced mushrooms, cucumbers,
           tomato and
    1 oz crumbled feta cheese, and
    5 large olives, topped with
    olive oil-vinegar-lemon dressing
1 sm whole-wheat pita pocket
1 med apple
iced tea or club soda

DINNER   tofu stir-fry:
    4 oz tofu, sliced thin, stir fried in
    1-2 tsp peanut oil; add
    1-2 cups mixed vegetables (celery,
        carrots, red cabbage, bamboo shoots,
        Chinese mushrooms, green beans, and
        bok choy); on bed of
        1 cup brown rice
1/2 cup pineapple tidbits
tea

SNACK   1/2 cup ice milk

DAY TEN

BREAKFAST   1/2 cup apple juice
1 cup bran cereal with
   1/4 cup sliced strawberries and
   1/2 cup skim or lowfat milk
herbal tea or coffee

LUNCH   peanut butter-banana sandwich:
   2 sl toasted oatmeal bread, with
      1-2 tsp peanut butter and
      1/2 sm banana, sliced thin
1 cup skim or lowfat milk
1 sm box (1-1/2 oz) raisins

DINNER   cherrystone clams (1 cup or 10-15) with
   fresh horseradish
tossed salad with
   lowfat avocado dressing
1 med ear corn-on-the-cob
1 sm slice sponge cake with
   1/4 cup raspberries and
1-2 Tbsp vanilla-flavored lowfat yogurt
iced tea or club soda

SNACK   2-3 cups popcorn with
   1 tsp grated Parmesan cheese

DAY ELEVEN

BREAKFAST 1/2 cup pineapple juice
1 cup hot oat bran cereal with
   1 Tbsp chopped dates and
   1/2 cup skim or lowfat milk
herbal tea or coffee

LUNCH seafood salad sandwich:
   3-1/2 oz canned salmon (or mackerel)
     mixed with
      1-2 Tbsp lowfat yogurt
      chopped onion
      celery
      carrot, and
      lettuce leaves on
   2 sl rye bread
1 cup skim or lowfat milk
1 med pear

DINNER 3 oz roasted lean lamb, with
   1/2 tsp mint jelly
1/2 lg sweet potato, baked and mashed
1/2 cup wild rice
1 cup steamed broccoli with pearl onions
1/2 cup fruit cocktail
iced tea or club soda

SNACK choco-shake:
1 cup skim or lowfat milk, blend with
   1 tsp cocoa and
   crushed ice, until smooth

DAY TWELVE

BREAKFAST 1 cup lowfat yogurt mixed with
    1/2 cup fresh berries (strawberries,
      raspberries, and/or blueberries) and
    1/2 sm sliced banana, and
    1 tsp wheat germ
1 sl toasted oatmeal bread, with
    1 tsp all-fruit preserve
herbal tea or coffee

LUNCH hummus sandwich:
    1/2 cup hummus in
    1 sm whole-wheat pita pocket with
      cucumber, tomato slices, and
      lettuce
1 cup skim or lowfat milk
fresh tangerine

DINNER 3-4 oz broiled haddock with lemon
1 med baked potato with
    1 Tbsp lowfat yogurt
1 cup steamed lima beans
1/2 cup boiled beets
1 light beer or club soda

SNACK 3-4 whole grain crackers
1-1/2 oz lowfat cheese
1/2 cup cider

DAY THIRTEEN

BREAKFAST 1/2 cup orange juice
1 cup oat bran flakes with
   1 sliced fresh peach, and
   1/2 cup skim or lowfat milk
herbal tea or coffee

LUNCH chef's salad:
   Bibb lettuce with
      1-2 oz lean chicken or turkey strips,
         and sliced cucumber, tomato, bell
         peppers and
      1-1/2 oz lowfat cheese strips, topped
         with lowfat Ranch-style dressing
   1 sm whole wheat roll
   1/2 cup pineapple chunks
   iced tea or club soda

DINNER lean burger:
   3 oz extra-lean, broiled ground beef, on
      1 whole grain bun with
      sliced onion and tomato, and lettuce
         leaves
   1 cup mixed vegetables (corn, peas,
      carrots), steamed
   1 cup skim or lowfat milk
   1/2 cup applesauce

SNACK 1/2 cup ice milk
1 oz peanuts or pecans, chopped

DAY FOURTEEN

BREAKFAST　1/2 med grapefruit
2 sm buckwheat pancakes with
　1-2 tsp pure maple syrup
1 cup skim or lowfat milk
herbal tea or coffee

LUNCH　muffin broiler:
　1 whole wheat English muffin, split;
　broil with
　　1-1/2 oz part-skim mozzarella cheese
　　and top with
　　1/4 tsp Dijon-style mustard
1 cup fruit salad
iced tea or club soda

DINNER　chicken with herbs:
　3 oz baked skinless chicken, with
　　sliced tomato, fresh basil, tarragon
tabouleh salad:
　1 cup cracked wheat with
　　chopped tomato, fresh mint, and
　　scant amount of olive oil
1 cup steamed zucchini with lemon
baked banana with honey
iced tea or club soda

SNACK　1/4 cup hummus with
　vegetable sticks (celery, carrots, bell
　　pepper, etc.)

DAY FIFTEEN

BREAKFAST　1/2 cup orange juice
1 cup oatmeal with
　　1 Tbsp raisins and
　　1/2 cup skim or lowfat milk
herbal tea or coffee

LUNCH　lobster salad:
　　3-1/2 oz chilled cooked lobster, on
　　　bed of lettuce with
　　　　sliced cucumbers and tomato, and
　　1-2 Tbsp lowfat yogurt (as dressing)
3-4 whole-grain sesame crackers
fresh peach
iced tea or club soda

DINNER　baked macaroni:
　　1 cup whole wheat macaroni, cooked,
　　　and mixed with
　　　　1-1/2 oz lowfat cheese
　　　　1/2 cup lowfat cottage cheese
　　　　2 tsp grated Parmesan cheese
　　　　season to taste
1 cup steamed broccoli with lemon
tossed salad with
　　lowfat Italian dressing
1-2 fresh apricots
iced tea or club soda

SNACK　1 cup lowfat yogurt with
　　1/4 cup crushed pineapple

DAY SIXTEEN

BREAKFAST 1/2 med grapefruit
1-2 sm oat bran muffins
1 cup skim or lowfat milk
herbal tea or coffee

LUNCH spinach salad:
    fresh spinach leaves with
        fresh mushroom slices,
        grated hard-cooked egg whites,
        1-2 sardines and
        lowfat Italian dressing
1-2 whole wheat breadsticks
1 med apple
iced tea or club soda

DINNER turkey stir-fry:
    3 oz turkey, cut in strips, stir fried in
        1-2 tsp peanut oil, with
    1-2 cups mixed vegetables (celery, red
        cabbage, zucchini, water chestnuts,
        peapods, mushrooms)
1 cup brown rice
1/2 cup fresh papaya
tea

SNACK 1 cup skim or lowfat milk
1-2 fig cookies

DAY SEVENTEEN

BREAKFAST 1/2 cup apple juice
1 cup bran cereal with
   1/2 sm banana, sliced, and
   1/2 cup skim or lowfat milk
herbal tea or coffee

LUNCH peanut butter sandwich:
   1 rye bagel, split, with
      1-2 tsp peanut butter
1 cup skim or lowfat milk
1 sm box (1-1/2 oz) raisins

DINNER jumbo shrimp cocktail:
   1/2 cup shrimp (5-6 large) with
      1 Tbsp fresh salsa
tossed salad with
   lowfat avocado dressing
1/2 cup steamed green beans with
   1 tsp slivered almonds
1 sm slice angelfood cake with
   1/4 cup blueberries
iced tea or club soda

SNACK 3-4 whole grain crackers with
   1 oz lowfat cheese

DAY EIGHTEEN

BREAKFAST   1/2 cup pineapple juice
1 cup hot oat bran cereal with
   1 Tbsp raisins and
   1/2 cup skim or lowfat milk
herbal tea or coffee

LUNCH   broiled tuna melt sandwich:
   3-1/2 oz canned tuna mixed with
      1-2 Tbsp lowfat yogurt
      onion powder
      garlic powder
      fresh parsley, on
   2 sl oatmeal toast, topped with
      1-1/2 oz part-skim mozzarella cheese,
1 med pear
iced tea or club soda

DINNER   3 oz lean pork roast
1/2 lg sweet potato, baked and mashed
1/2 cup winter squash, baked and mashed
1 cup steamed cauliflower with lemon
1 sm whole wheat roll
4 oz dry red wine or club soda with lime

SNACK   yogurt shake:
   1 cup plain lowfat yogurt, blend with
      1/2 cup fresh fruit (berries, banana,
        and/or peach) and crushed ice, until
        smooth

DAY NINETEEN

BREAKFAST 1/4 med cantaloupe filled with
    1/2 cup lowfat cottage cheese
    10-12 fresh cherries, pitted and sliced
1 sl toasted oatmeal bread, with
    1 tsp marmalade or all-fruit preserve
herbal tea or coffee

LUNCH 1 cup meatless chili with
    1 tsp grated Parmesan cheese
3-4 whole wheat crackers
fresh tangerine
iced tea or club soda

DINNER 3-4 oz broiled cod with
    sliced tomato, fresh parsley
1 med red potato, baked
1 cup corn niblets
tossed salad with
    lowfat Thousand Island dressing
1 cup skim or lowfat milk

SNACK 1 cup lowfat yogurt (vanilla, coffee or
    lemon-flavored)
1-2 graham crackers

DAY TWENTY

BREAKFAST   1/2 cup orange juice
1 cup oat bran flakes with
 1/2 sm banana, sliced, and
 1/2 cup skim or lowfat milk
herbal tea or coffee

LUNCH   3 bean salad:
 Romaine lettuce bed with
  1/2 cup chickpeas, kidney beans,
  white beans, and
  1/2 cup lowfat cottage cheese, dress
  with olive oil-vinegar-lemon juice
1-2 whole wheat breadsticks
1/2 cup fresh mangos
iced tea or club soda

DINNER   3 oz baked chicken
1 med potato, baked and mashed
1 cup steamed carrots
1/2 cup sweet peas with pearl onions
baked apple with honey and raisins
iced tea or club soda

SNACK   1 cup skim or lowfat milk
1 sm bran muffin

DAY TWENTY-ONE

BREAKFAST   1/2 med grapefruit
1 egg, poached, on
   1 sl oatmeal toast
1 cup skim or lowfat milk
herbal tea or coffee

LUNCH   broiled pocket pizza:
   1 sm whole-wheat pita stuffed with
      1-1/2 oz part-skim mozzarella cheese
      and
      1 med sliced tomato
1 cup fruit salad
iced tea or club soda

DINNER   black beans 'n rice:
   1 cup cooked black beans, with
      1 cup cooked brown rice,
      sauteed onion
      garlic
      mushrooms
tossed salad with
   lowfat avocado dressing
nectarine
iced tea or club soda

SNACK   vegetable crunchies (raw carrot, celery,
   zucchini sticks)
1/2 cup lowfat yogurt with lemon and
   chives (as dip)

DAY TWENTY-TWO

BREAKFAST 1/2 cup orange juice
1 cup oatmeal with
   1 Tbsp chopped dates and
   1/2 cup skim or lowfat milk
herbal tea or coffee

LUNCH crab salad:
   1/2 cup chilled cooked crab, (fresh or
   canned) on bed of lettuce with
     sliced cucumbers, cherry tomatoes,
     and dressed with
     1-2 Tbsp lowfat yogurt
3-4 whole grain-sesame crackers
fresh peach
iced tea or club salad

DINNER 1 cup cooked whole wheat lasagna, bake
  with
    1-1/2 oz lowfat cheese
    1/2 cup lowfat ricotta cheese
    1/2 cup chopped spinach
    1/2 cup tomato sauce (made with
     olive oil)
tossed green salad with
   lowfat Italian dressing
4 oz dry red wine or club soda with lemon

SNACK 1/2 cup ice milk
1/4 cup berries (strawberries, blueberries,
  and/or raspberries)

DAY TWENTY-THREE

BREAKFAST   1/2 med grapefruit
1-2 sm oat bran muffins
1 cup skim or lowfat milk
herbal tea or coffee

LUNCH   salad nicoise:
Romaine lettuce tossed with
3-1/2 oz canned tuna
wedges of tomato
1/2 cup white beans
1 sm boiled potato, cut in wedges,
topped with
lowfat Italian dressing
1-2 whole grain breadsticks
1 med apple
iced tea or club soda

DINNER   tofu stir-fry:
4 oz tofu, sliced thin, stir-fried in
1-2 tsp peanut oil, add
1-2 cups mixed vegetables (carrots,
bamboo shoots, Chinese mushrooms,
green beans, and bok choy)
1 cup brown rice
1/2 cup pineapple tidbits
tea

SNACK   1 cup skim or lowfat milk
1-2 oatmeal-raisin cookies

DAY TWENTY-FOUR

BREAKFAST 1/2 cup applejuice
1 cup bran cereal with
    1/4 cup sliced strawberries
    1/2 cup skim or lowfat milk
herbal tea or coffee

LUNCH peanut butter and raisin sandwich:
    2 sl oatmeal bread with
        1-2 tsp peanut butter
        1 Tbsp raisins
1 cup skim or lowfat milk
1 sm banana

DINNER 3-4 oz broiled scallops with lemon
1/2 cup acorn squash, baked and mashed
1/2 cup steamed wax beans
tossed salad with
    lowfat French dressing
1/2 pear, poached in red wine
iced tea or club soda

SNACK 2-3 cups popcorn with
    1 tsp grated Parmesan cheese

DAY TWENTY-FIVE

BREAKFAST
1/2 cup pineapple juice
1 cup hot oat bran cereal with
   1 Tbsp chopped dates
   1/2 cup skim or lowfat milk
herbal tea or coffee

LUNCH
salmon salad sandwich:
   3-1/2 oz canned salmon mixed with
      1-2 Tbsp lowfat yogurt
      chopped onion
      celery
      red bell peppers, and
      lettuce leaves on
   2 sl cracked wheat bread
1 cup skim or lowfat milk
1 med pear

DINNER
3 oz broiled lean sirloin
1 med baked potato
1/2 cup steamed brussel sprouts
1/2 cup corn niblets
1 sm whole wheat roll
1 cup fresh fruit salad
iced tea or club soda

SNACK

1/2 cup ice milk
1 oz chopped cashews or filberts

DAY TWENTY-SIX

BREAKFAST   1 cup lowfat yogurt mixed with
        1/2 cup fresh berries (strawberries,
          raspberries, and/or blueberries)
        1/2 sm sliced banana
        1 tsp wheat germ
      1 sl oatmeal bread, toasted, with
        1 tsp all-fruit preserve
      herbal tea or coffee

LUNCH   broiled avocado sandwich:
        1 sm whole-wheat pita pocket, stuffed
          with
          1/2 avocado, peeled and sliced
          1-1/2 oz lowfat cheese
          sliced tomato
          sprouts
      fresh tangerine
      iced tea or club soda

DINNER   3-4 oz broiled bluefish or lake trout
      1 med baked red potato
      1 cup steamed broccoli with lemon
      tossed salad with
        lowfat Ranch-style dressing
      3 oz dry white wine or club soda

SNACK   1 cup skim or lowfat milk
      1-2 oatmeal-raisin cookies

DAY TWENTY-SEVEN

BREAKFAST 1/2 cup orange juice
1 cup oat bran flakes with
   1 fresh peach, sliced
   1/2 cup skim or lowfat milk
herbal tea or coffee

LUNCH antipasto salad:
   iceberg lettuce bed with
      1-1/2 oz part-skim mozzarella cheese
       strips
      1 oz turkey "ham" strips
      sliced cucumber
      tomato wedges
      5 lg Greek olives
      2 anchovies, topped with
      lowfat Italian dressing
1-2 whole grain breadsticks
fresh plum
iced tea or club soda

DINNER 3 oz baked chicken
1/2 cup barley stuffing (made without
   egg yolk or butter)
1 cup steamed baby carrots with fresh mint
   garnish
1/2 cup baby sweet peas
baked apple with honey and raisins
iced tea or club soda

SNACK 2 rice cakes with
   1 oz lowfat cheese

DAY TWENTY-EIGHT

BREAKFAST   1/2 med grapefruit
1 med whole wheat waffle with
    1-2 tsp pure maple syrup
1 cup skim or lowfat milk
herbal tea or coffee

LUNCH   muffin broiler:
    1 whole wheat English muffin, split,
        topped with
            1-1/2 oz part-skim mozzarella cheese
            thinly sliced mushrooms, onion, and
                green pepper
1 cup fruit salad
iced tea or club soda

DINNER   meatless chili
tossed salad with
    lowfat avocado dressing
1 sm whole wheat roll
nectarine
iced tea or club soda

SNACK   1 cup lowfat yogurt (vanilla, lemon, or
coffee-flavored)

DAY TWENTY-NINE

BREAKFAST 1/2 cup orange juice
1-2 sm oat bran muffins
1 cup skim or lowfat milk
herbal tea or coffee

LUNCH 2 herrings in tomato sauce
lg tossed salad with
    lowfat Italian dressing
1/2 cup lowfat cottage cheese
1 sm whole grain roll
1 cup melon balls
iced tea or club soda

DINNER 1 cup baked beans with
    1 oz sliced chicken "hot dogs"
1 sl brown bread (or pumpernickel)
1 med ear corn-on-the-cob
1 cup steamed greens (turnip, mustard,
    kale) with fresh lemon slices
1/2 cup applesauce
iced tea or club soda

SNACK 1 cup skim or lowfat milk
1/2 whole wheat English muffin with
    1 tsp all-fruit preserve

DAY THIRTY

BREAKFAST 1 cup citrus selections (orange and
  grapefruit)
1 egg, soft-boiled
1 sl toasted oatmeal bread
herbal tea or coffee

LUNCH 1 cup low-sodium bean soup (lentil or split
  pea)
3-4 whole rye crackers
1 cup skim or lowfat milk
1-2 fig cookies

DINNER steamed mussels (1-2 cups) in
  tomato sauce (made with olive oil)
1 thick sl Italian bread
1 cup steamed Italian-cut beans
tossed salad with
  lowfat avocado dressing
1 sm fresh persimmon
iced tea or club soda

SNACK 1 cup skim or lowfat milk
1/2 whole wheat English muffin with
  1 tsp all-fruit preserve

IMPORTANT NOTES

* Frozen or canned fruits should be packed in their own juices — without added sugar or syrup.

* Vegetables should be fresh or frozen without added salt or sauces; low-sodium canned are acceptable alternatives.

* Breads and cereals should be whole grain products.

* Whole-grain pastas and brown rice are preferred.

* Crackers and breadsticks should be whole grain and *unsalted*.

* Prepare popcorn without added oil, butter, or salt by using hot-air popper or oil-free microwave popcorn.

* Prepare dried beans and peas by soaking overnight in cold water before cooking; read labels on canned beans to check for (and avoid) added salt and fats.

* Peanut butter should be old-fashioned or natural brands made without added hydrogenated fats or salt; nuts should be *unsalted*.

* Fish should be prepared by baking, boiling, broiling, or poaching; brush with olive oil (lightly) and season with herbs, if desired.

* Canned fish should be low-sodium when possible.

* Poultry should be skinless and prepared by baking, boiling, broiling, or roasting; dark meat is significantly lower in fat than white meat.

* Meats should be lean, well-trimmed, and prepared by baking, boiling, broiling, or roasting; use small amounts of lean cuts to *complement* the meal, rather than serving meat as the main dish.

* Limit egg intake to 1-2 yolks weekly; use egg whites to stretch recipes (1 whole egg + 1 egg white for 2 whole eggs) or use egg substitutes (read labels to ensure products are no-cholesterol and low-sodium choices).

* Select skim or lowfat (1%) milk, nonfat or lowfat yogurt, and un-creamed or lowfat (1% or 2%) cottage cheese.

* Select lowfat cheeses (less than 3 grams fat/oz) by reading labels; use *light* dustings of grated Parmesan cheese to add flavor (and nutrition) to vegetables and casserole-type dishes.

* Use *small* amounts of olive oil with vinegar and lemon to dress salads, or choose olive oil-based salad dressings — and use *sparingly*; low-calorie, low-fat, and fat-free salad dressings are preferred.

* Soups, chili, and tomato sauce should be homemade, or carefully
  selected from available products made without fats (or including only olive oil) and low in sodium.
* Oat bran muffins should be homemade, or prepared commercial-
  ly without egg yolk, butter or shortening.
* Occasional sweets or treats may help to prevent the psychological
  depression that often triggers eating binges and "blown" diets.
* Light beers and dry wines are the best choices for alcoholic
  beverages — for those who drink; nonalcoholic beers and wines
  are also available.
* Occasional servings of foods that are *not* low in cholesterol, sodium,
  and/or calories can be included (as in the sample menus) in
  MODERATE AMOUNTS to add variety, flavor, psychological ap-
  peal, and eating enjoyment to your diet.

Remember, moderation is the key to eating for good health!

DINING OUT
DO'S AND DON'TS

Just because you are being careful in your food selections, you
do not have to give up restaurants altogether, nor opt for brown bag
lunches every day. By following a few basic guidelines, you can make
wise food choices almost *anywhere* — whether at a fast food outlet, a
business luncheon, or a friend's dinner table. In order to make menu
selections that can help lower your cholesterol while you lose weight,
keep in mind the following suggestions:

	Do's	**Don'ts**
APPETIZERS:	fresh vegetables	soups or broths
	fresh fruits	salted crackers
	fresh fruit juices	chips, dips, etc.
	oysters or clams	caviar
	shrimp cocktail	cocktail sauce

	Do's	**Don'ts**

SALADS:	green, tossed
	chef's with poultry,
	  lean meats (no egg)
	spinach with
	  anchovies (no egg)
	oil-based dressing
	olive oil
		mayonnaise-based
		potato salad
		egg salad
		creamy coleslaw
		creamy or cheese
		  dressing

Note: request that dressing be served on the side

	Do's	**Don'ts**
BREADS & MUFFINS:	pumpernickel, rye, oatmeal, whole grain, whole wheat, cracked wheat, bran, oat bran: breads, bagels rolls, muffins, pita and English muffins	garlic bread buttered breads and rolls egg or cheese bread crackers, salted biscuits sweet rolls breadsticks, salted

MEATS:	lean, well-trimmed—
	baked, boiled, or
	roasted
		breaded or fried
		  marinated, gravies,
		  sauces, stews

POULTRY:	chicken or turkey,
	light meat, no skin—
	baked, boiled, broiled,
	or roasted
		goose, duck
		  breaded or fried
		  marinated, gravies,
		  sauces, stews

FISH:	cold water (cod, lake
	trout, mackerel,
	swordfish, tuna,
	bluefish, salmon)
	shellfish (clams, crab,
	lobsters, mussels,
	oysters, scallops,
	shrimp)
	sardines, anchovies,
	herring, white fish
	(haddock, flounder, etc.)
		breaded, fried
		  dried or smoked,
		  pickled
		fishsticks
		sauces, cocktail sauce
		chowders or stews

	Do's	Don'ts
LUNCHEON MEATS:	lean turkey products (turkey "ham") lean chicken products (chicken "hot dogs") extra lean hamburgers peanut butter (moderate amounts) tofu	bacon bologna hot dogs, burgers sausages, salami ham
VEGETABLES:	dried beans and peas raw or steamed stir-fried (in olive or peanut oil)	buttered, creamed or deep fried sauces
DESSERTS:	fruit—fresh, baked, or poached frozen fruit ice, sorbet lowfat yogurt, frozen lowfat yogurt angelfood cake, sponge cake	rich sweets—cakes ice cream, pies, pastries, cookies, candy
BEVERAGES:	fruit juice skim, lowfat milk coffee, tea, herbal tea light beers dry wines club soda, carbonated waters	tomato juice, vegetable cocktails whole milk, cream, cream substitutes sweetened drinks, soft drinks, liqueurs, or tonic water
EXTRAS:	*in moderate amounts* olive oil, olives avocado peanut oil oat bran products almonds, cashews, filberts chickpeas, kidney beans, soybeans, tofu	mayonnaise sour cream pickles, relish catsup MSG (monosodium glutamate) bacon bits whipped cream

ADDITIONAL NOTES: Avoid menu selections described as:
* buttered, buttery, in butter sauce
* creamed, creamy, in cream sauce
* crispy, extra crispy
* fried, french fried, pan fried, deep-fried
* in cheese sauce, au gratin, parmigiana
* escalloped, a la king
* bearnaise, Hollandaise, special sauce
* casserole, pot pie, stew
* pickled, smoked tenderized
* all you can eat

HOW TO USE THE FOOD VALUE LISTS

Use the following food value lists to make your dieting simpler. Whenever you eat you can use these lists to determine the approximate per serving amounts of CHOLESTEROL, SODIUM, and CALORIES.

The food values provided in these lists were adapted from the latest figures given by the United States Department of Agriculture. Remember, however, that these values are only *estimates*! Variability in size, season, storage and preparation, plus inaccuracies in computations and determinations must be taken into account. Think of it this way:

> You have eaten an apple. Using the FOOD VALUE LIST you determined it contains 61 calories. But was that apple *exactly* 2-1/2 inches in diameter? Was it a sweet, ripe variety or a sour type of apple? Was it fresh off the tree in your yard, or did you purchase it several days ago at the local supermarket? And did you eat *every bit* of edible fruit? And if the apple was eaten as Apple Brown Betty, the specific recipe would have to be considered. After all, homemade Apple Brown Betty is certainly different from the one served in restaurants or from your friend's recipe.

Manufacturers are constantly altering food products. Food

labels can usually provide the most current information on calorie and nutrient contents. This can be especially helpful with those products not included in the food value lists. And, if portion sizes given in the lists differ from actual portion sizes eaten, estimates can be made using the COMMON MEASUREMENTS CONVERSION TABLE in the APPENDIX. A METRIC CONVERSION TABLE is also included in the APPENDIX.

Obviously, exact food values are impossible for you to determine, and impractical for you to be concerned over. The approximate food values, however, can be of great assistance in determining your average daily intake of CHOLESTEROL, SODIUM, and CALORIES.

The FOOD VALUE LIST provides the approximate amounts of CHOLESTEROL, SODIUM, and CALORIES in common servings of typical foods in alphabetical order.

The food value lists also can assist you in planning your meals in advance. Use the MENU PLANNING LISTS to devise menus for well-balanced, nutritious meals and snacks. The approximate amounts of CHOLESTEROL, SODIUM, and CALORIES in common servings of typical foods are listed under several headings:

LOW-CAL BREAKFAST FOODS

LOW-CAL LUNCH and DINNER FOODS

LOW-CAL SNACKS

One serving of each item in these sections contains no more than 10 grams of CHOLESTEROL, 150 milligrams of SODIUM, and 150 CALORIES.

The LOW-CAL BEVERAGES section lists a variety of nutritious liquids. One serving of each beverage contains no more than 10 *grams* of CHOLESTEROL, 150 *milligrams* of SODIUM, and 120 CALORIES.

A special list also is included providing the food values for the BREAKFAST, LUNCH, DINNER and SNACK PROTEIN FOODS. Some of these foods are not as low in CHOLESTEROL, SODIUM, and CALORIES as the items included in the other sections, but one serving of each provides generous amounts of protein with no more than 80 *grams* of CHOLESTEROL, 200 *milligrams* of SODIUM, and 200 CALORIES.

A second special list has been included which provides the food values for selections that can help lower blood cholesterol levels. The CHOLESTEROL-REDUCING FOODS may not be as low in SODIUM, and CALORIES as the items in the preceding five sections, but one serving of each provides no more than 200 calories PLUS special food factors to reduce elevated blood cholesterol.

So, good luck! Hopefully, these food value lists will provide you with the information you need to eat healthfully and enjoyably while you cure your cholesterol (and weight) woes.

The following abbreviations are used in the counters:

av	= average size	pkg	= package
cals	= calories	sl	= slice
chol	= cholesterol	sm	= small
cu in	= cubic inch	sod	= sodium
dia	= diameter	sq	= square
lb	= pound	t	= trace amount
lg	= large	Tbsp	= tablespoon
med	= medium-sized	tsp	= teaspoon
mg	= milligrams	"	= inch
mini	= miniature	"−"	= an unknown value
oz	= ounce		

ADDITIONAL NOTES: The food values given in the counters reflect the following:

* All flour is enriched.
* All cornmeal is degermed & enriched.
* All canned fruits and vegetables are drained.
* A measured cup is spooned in, rather than packed.
* Unless otherwise noted, products are medium sized.
* "Homemade" items were made according to the U.S. Department of Agriculture's own standardized recipes.

FOOD	AMOUNT	CAL	CHOL (mg.)	SOD (mg.)

FOOD VALUE LIST

A

FOOD	AMOUNT	CAL	CHOL (mg.)	SOD (mg.)
Almonds:				
dried, shelled, chopped	1 Tbsp.	48	0	t
roasted, salted	1 cup	984	0	311
shelled, slivered	1 cup	688	0	5
Almond meal, partially defatted	1 oz.	116	0	2
Amaranth leaves, fresh	1 lb.	163	0	—
Anchovies, canned, 4" long	5	35	20	—
Apple Brown Betty	1 cup	325	t	329
Apple butter	1 Tbsp.	33	0	t
Apples:				
dehydrated, uncooked	1 cup	353	0	7
dried, rings	1 cup	234	0	4
fresh, whole, 3" dia.	1	96	0	2
fresh, whole, 2-1/2" dia.	1	61	0	1
juice, canned or bottled	1 cup	117	0	2
Applesauce:				
canned, sweetened	1 cup	232	0	5
canned, unsweetened	1 cup	100	0	5
Apricots:				
canned, sweetened	1 cup	222	0	3
canned, unsweetened	1 cup	93	0	2
dehydrated, uncooked	1 cup	332	0	33
dried, uncooked	1 cup	338	0	34
fresh, halves	1 cup	79	0	2
fresh, whole	3	55	0	1
nectar, canned or bottled (40% fruit)	1 cup	143	0	1
Artichokes:				
French or globe, cooked	1 bud	16	0	36
Jerusalem, pared, cooked	4 oz.	75	0	2

FOOD	AMOUNT	CAL	CHOL (mg.)	SOD (mg.)
Asparagus:				
canned, spears	1 cup	51	0	571
fresh, cuts	1 cup	35	0	3
fresh, cuts, cooked	1 cup	29	0	1
fresh, spears, cooked	1 cup	36	0	2
Avocados:				
California, 3-1/8" dia.	1	369	0	9
Florida, 3-5/8" dia.	1	389	0	12
frozen, cuts, cooked	1 cup	44	0	2
frozen, spears, cooked	1 cup	40	0	2

B

FOOD	AMOUNT	CAL	CHOL (mg.)	SOD (mg.)
Bacon:				
Canadian, cooked	1 sl.	58	30	537
cured, cooked	1 sl.	43	15	76
Baking powder:				
phosphate	1 tsp.	5	0	312
sodium aluminum sulfate	1 tsp.	3	0	323
special low sodium	1 tsp.	7	0	t
tartrate	1 tsp.	2	0	204
Bamboo shoots, fresh	1 cup	41	0	1
Bananas:				
baking (see Plantain)				
dehydrated, flakes	1 cup	340	0	4
fresh, 9-3/4" long	1	116	0	1
fresh, 8-3/4" long	1	101	0	1
fresh, 7-3/4" long	1	81	0	1
fresh, mashed	1 cup	191	0	2
fresh, sliced	1 cup	128	0	2
Barbeque sauce	1 cup	228	0	2,038
Barley, pearled:				
light, uncooked	1 cup	698	0	6
pot or Scotch, uncooked	1 cup	696	0	12
Bass, fresh oven-fried	4 oz.	224	75	77
Bean curd (see Soybeans)				
Beans:				
dry, pinto, uncooked	1 cup	663	0	19

FOOD	AMOUNT	CAL	CHOL (mg.)	SOD (mg.)
dry, red kidney, cooked	1 cup	218	0	6
dry, white, Great Norther, cooked	1 cup	212	0	13
dry, white, Navy (pea), cooked .	1 cup	224	0	13
dry, white, with meat and molasses	1 cup	383	0	969
dry, white, with meat and tomato sauce	1 cup	311	0	1,181
dry, white, with meatless tomato sauce	1 cup	306	0	862
green or snap, canned	1 cup	32	0	319
green or snap, fresh	1 cup	35	0	8
green or snap, fresh, cooked . .	1 cup	31	0	5
green or snap, frozen, cooked .	1 cup	34	0	1
French style, canned	1 cup	31	0	307
French style, frozen, cooked . .	1 cup	34	0	3
lima, canned	1 cup	163	0	401
lima, fresh, cooked	1 cup	189	0	2
lima, frozen, cooked ("baby") . .	1 cup	212	0	232
lima, frozen, cooked ("fordhook")	1 cup	168	0	172
sprouts, mung	1 cup	37	0	5
sprouts, mung, cooked	1 cup	35	0	5
yellow or wax, canned	1 cup	32	0	319
yellow or wax, fresh	1 cup	30	0	8
yellow or wax, fresh, cooked . .	1 cup	28	0	4
yellow or wax, frozen, cooked .	1 cup	36	0	1
Bean Sprouts (see Beans, Soybeans)				
Beans and franks, canned	1 cup	367	25	1,374
Beechnuts, shelled	1 oz.	161	0	—
Beef, lean, trimmed, cooked:				
boneless chuck for stew	1 cup	300	109	74
chuck, rib roast or steak, choice grade	3 oz.	212	77	43
chuck, rib roast or steak, good grade	3 oz.	186	77	44
chuck roast or steak, choice grade	3 oz.	164	77	45

FOOD	AMOUNT	CAL	CHOL (mg.)	SOD (mg.)
chuck roast or steak,				
good grade	3 oz.	152	77	46
flank steak (London broil)	3 oz.	167	77	45
ground, 10% fat	3 oz.	186	77	57
ground, 21% fat	3 oz.	259	77	54
loin, clubsteak	4 oz.	515	90	57
loin, porterhouse steak	4 oz.	254	90	84
loin, t-bone steak	4 oz.	253	90	85
plate beef	4 oz.	226	90	60
rib roast	3 oz.	205	77	59
round steak	3 oz.	161	77	65
rump roast, choice grade	3 oz.	177	77	61
rump roast, good grade	3 oz.	162	77	62
sirloin, double-bone	3 oz.	184	77	64
sirloin, hipbone	3 oz.	204	77	62
sirloin, wedge-and round-bone	3 oz.	176	77	67
Beef and vegetable stew, canned	1 cup	194	36	1,007
Beef, corned:				
canned, cooked	4 oz.	245	103	1,480
canned, hash	1 cup	398	120	1,188
fresh, cooked	4 oz.	422	103	1,069
Beef, dried:				
chipped, creamed	1 cup	377	65	1,754
chipped, uncooked	1 oz.	58	–	1,219
Beef pot pie, homemade, 9" dia.	1/3 pie	517	44	596
Beer (see Beverages)				
Beet greens, cooked	1 cup	26	0	110
Beets:				
canned, diced or sliced	1 cup	63	0	401
canned, whole, small	1 cup	59	0	378
fresh, diced or sliced, cooked	1 cup	54	0	73
fresh, whole, 2" dia., cooked	2	32	0	43
Harvard	1 cup	80	0	–
pickled	1 cup	80	0	756
Beverages, alcoholic:				
ale (7% alcohol)	12 oz.	168	0	15
beer (4.5% alcohol)	12 oz.	151	0	25
beer "light"	12 oz.	96	0	–

FOOD	AMOUNT	CAL	CHOL (mg.)	SOD (mg.)
gin, rum, vodka, whiskey				
(86 proof)	1-1/2 oz.	105	0	t
(100 proof)	1-1/2 oz.	124	0	t
wine, dessert				
(18.8% alcohol)	3-1/2 oz.	141	0	4
table(12% alcohol)	3-1/2 oz.	87	0	5
Beverages, carbonated*:				
club soda, unsweetened	12 oz.	0	0	39
cola	12 oz.	144	0	3-49
cream soda	12 oz.	160	0	4
fruit flavored sodas	12 oz.	171	0	7-81
ginger ale	12 oz.	113	0	7-28
root beer	12 oz.	152	0	3-38
special "diet" sodas	12 oz.	0-12	0	—
Tom Collins mixer	12 oz.	171	0	17
tonic water	12 oz.	113	0	19

depends on sodium content of water supply at bottling plant

FOOD	AMOUNT	CAL	CHOL (mg.)	SOD (mg.)
Biscuit, baking powder:				
from mix, 2" dia.	1	91	t	272
homemade, 2" dia.	1	103	t	175
Blackberries:				
canned, sweetened	1 cup	233	0	3
canned, unsweetened	1 cup	98	0	2
*fresh	1 cup	84	0	1
**frozen, sweetened	1 cup	60	0	1
**frozen, unsweetened	1 cup	137	0	1
juice, canned, unsweetened . .	1 cup	91	0	2

includes dewberries, boysenberries, young berries
**includes boysenberries*

Blackeye peas (see Cowpeas)

Blood pudding (see Sausage)

FOOD	AMOUNT	CAL	CHOL (mg.)	SOD (mg.)
Blueberries:				
fresh	1 cup	90	0	1
frozen, sweetened	1 cup	242	0	2
frozen, unsweetened	1 cup	91	0	2
Bluefish:				
fresh, baked with margarine . . .	4 oz.	185	63	118
fried fillet, 8-1/8" long	1 fillet	400	84	285

FOOD	AMOUNT	CAL	CHOL (mg.)	SOD (mg.)
Bockwurst (see Sausage)				
Bologna (see Cold Cuts)				
Boston brown bread, canned, 1/2" thick	1 sl.	95	0	113
Bouillon, instant:				
cube	1	5	t	960
powder	1 tsp.	2	t	480
Boysenberries (see Blackberries)				
Bran (see Cereals)				
Braunschweiger (see Sausage)				
Brazil nuts:				
shelled, large	1 cup	916	0	1
shelled, large	6	185	0	t
Bread:				
cracked wheat	1 sl.	66	t	132
French (2-1/2"x2"x1/2")	1 sl.	44	t	87
Italian (4-1/2"x3-1/4"x3/4")	1 sl.	83	t	176
pumpernickel	1 sl.	79	t	182
pumpernickel, party-size	1 sl.	17	t	40
raisin	1 sl.	66	t	91
regular	1 sl.	63	t	114
rye	1 sl.	61	t	139
rye, party-size	1 sl.	17	t	39
white, firm-crumb, thin	1 sl.	41	t	74
white, soft-crumb	1 sl.	76	t	142
whole wheat, firm-crumb	1 sl.	61	t	132
whole wheat, soft-crumb	1 sl.	67	t	148
Bread crumbs:				
dry, grated	1 cup	392	t	736
soft, cubed	1 cup	81	t	152
Bread pudding, with raisins	1 cup	496	64	533
Bread sticks, 4-1/2" long	1	38	t	70
Bread stuffing:				
mix, dry, crumbs	1 cup	260	t	932
prepared, crumbly	1 cup	501	t	1,254
prepared, moist	1 cup	416	t	1,008
Breakfast cereals (see Cereals)				

FOOD	AMOUNT	CAL	CHOL (mg.)	SOD (mg.)
Broadbeans, dry, raw . . . . 1 oz.		96	0	—
Broccoli:				
fresh, cuts, cooked . . . . 1 cup		40	0	16
fresh, stalks . . . . 1 med.		47	0	18
frozen, chopped, cooked . . . . 1 cup		48	0	28
frozen, stalks, cooked . . . . . 8 med.		65	0	30
Brownies (see Cookies)				
Brussels sprouts:				
fresh, cooked . . . . 1 cup		56	0	16
frozen, cooked . . . . 1 cup		51	0	22
Buckwheat (see Flour)				
Bulgur:				
canned, seasoned . . . . 1 cup		246	0	621
canned, unseasoned . . . . . . 1 cup		227	0	809
dry, from club wheat . . . . . 1 cup		628	0	—
dry, from hard red wheat . . . 1 cup		602	0	—
dry, from winter wheat . . . . 1 cup		553	0	—
Butter:				
regular type . . . . 1 stick		812	248	937
regular type . . . . 1 Tbsp.		102	35	117
regular type . . . . 1 pat		36	12	41
whipped type . . . . 1 Tbsp.		67	22	80
Buttermilk (see Milk)				
Butternuts, shelled . . . . 1 oz.		178	0	—

C

FOOD	AMOUNT	CAL	CHOL (mg.)	SOD (mg.)
Cabbage:				
Chinese, chopped . . . . 1 cup		11	0	17
red, chopped . . . . 1 cup		28	0	23
savoy, sliced . . . . 1 cup		17	0	15
spoon (pakchoy) chopped,				
cooked . . . . 1 cup		24	0	31
white, chopped . . . . 1 cup		22	0	18
white, wedges, cooked . . . . . 1 cup		31	0	22
Cabbage salad (see Coleslaw)				
Cake, from mix:				
Angelfood, cube . . . . 1 cu. in.		6	0	3

FOOD	AMOUNT	CAL	CHOL (mg.)	SOD (mg.)
9-3/4" dia.	2-1/2" arc	137	0	77
chocolate, white icing,				
9" dia.	1-3/4" arc	232	33	213
coffeecake, 7-3/4"x5-5/8" . .	1/16 cake	232	20	310
cupcake, uniced, 2-1/2" dia.	1	88	10	113
cupcake, chocolate icing,				
2-1/2 dia.	1	129	10	121
devil's food, chocolate icing,				
9" dia.	1-3/4" arc	234	33	181
gingerbread, 8-1/4" dia. . . .	2-3/4" sq.	174	t	192
marble, white icing, 9" dia. .	1-3/4" arc	215	33	168
spice, caramel icing,				
9" dia.	1-3/4" arc	271	33	189
white, chocolate icing				
9" dia.	1-3/4" arc	249	1	161
yellow, chocolate icing				
9" dia.	1-3/4" arc	233	36	157
Cakes, frozen:				
devil's food, choc. icing,				
7-1/2"x1-3/4"	4" sq.	323	36	357
Cake, homemade:				
Boston cream pie, 8" dia. . .	2-1/8" arc.	208	80	128
cottage pudding, 2"x4"	1 sl.	186	48	161
fruitcake, dark 7" tube	2/3" arc	163	7	68
fruitcake, light, 7" tube	2/3" arc	167	7	83
pound, 3-1/2"x3"x1/2"	1 sl.	142	20	33
sponge, 9-3/4" tube	2-1/2" arc.	131	162	73
Cake icings:				
from mix, chocolate	1 Tbsp.	79	t	30
homemade, carmel	1 Tbsp.	77	0	18
homemade, chocolate	1 Tbsp.	65	t	11
uncooked white	1 Tbsp.	75	0	10
Candied fruits (see individual kinds)				
Candy:				
butterscotch	1 oz.	113	t	19
candycorn	1 cup	728	0	424
caramels, plain or chocolate . . .	1 oz.	113	t	64
caramels, with nuts	1 oz.	121	t	58

FOOD	AMOUNT	CAL	CHOL (mg.)	SOD (mg.)
chocolate, bittersweet	1 oz.	135	40	1
chocolate, semi-sweet	1 oz.	144	40	1
chocolate, sweet	1 oz.	150	40	9
chocolate, milk, plain	1 oz.	147	50	27
chocolate, milk, with almonds . .	1 oz.	151	50	23
chocolate, milk, with peanuts . . .	1 oz.	154	50	19
chocolate-coated almonds	1 oz.	161	50	17
chocolate-coated coconut	1 oz.	124	20	56
chocolate-coated mints, 2-1/2" dia.	1 oz.	144	20	65
chocolate-coated fudge, caramel, peanuts	1 oz.	123	20	58
chocolate-coated honeycomb, peanut butter	1 oz.	131	20	46
chocolate-coated noughat, caramel	1 oz.	118	20	49
chocolate-coated peanuts	1 oz.	159	20	17
chocolate-coated raisins	1 oz.	120	20	18
chocolate-coated vanilla creams	1 oz.	123	40	52
fudge, chocolate	1 cu. in.	84	20	40
fudge, chocolate with nuts . .	1 cu. in.	89	20	36
fudge, vanilla	1 cu. in.	84	20	44
gumdrops	1 oz.	98	0	10
hard	1 oz.	109	0	9
jellybeans	10	104	0	3
marshmallows, large 1-1/8" dia.	1	23	0	3
marshmallows, mini 1/2" dia. . .	1 cup	147	0	18
mints, round, 1-1/2" dia.	1	32	0	19
mints, square, 5/8"x5/8"	1 cup	400	0	233
peanut bars	1 oz.	146	t	3
peanut brittle	1 oz.	119	t	9
sugar coated almonds	1 oz.	129	0	6
sugar coated chocolate disks . . .	1 oz.	132	50	20
Cantaloupe, fresh:				
5" dia.	1/2	82	0	33
diced	1 cup	48	0	19
Capicola (see Cold Cuts)				
Carob flour (see Flour)				

FOOD	AMOUNT	CAL	CHOL (mg.)	SOD (mg.)
Carrots:				
canned, diced	1 cup	44	0	342
canned, sliced	1 cup	47	0	366
fresh, 7" long	1	30	0	34
fresh, grated	1 cup	46	0	52
fresh, diced, cooked	1 cup	45	0	48
fresh, sliced, cooked	1 cup	48	0	51
Casaba melon, fresh:				
7-3/4" long	1/10	38	0	17
diced or balls	1 cup	46	0	20
Cashew nuts, roasted	1 cup	785	0	21
Catsup, tomato, bottled	1 Tbsp.	16	0	156
Cauliflower:				
fresh, whole buds	1 cup	27	0	13
fresh, cooked	1 cup	28	0	11
frozen, cooked	1 cup	32	0	18
Caviar, sturgeon:				
granular	1 Tbsp.	42	48*	352
pressed	1 Tbsp.	54	48*	—
Value is actually greater than 48				
Celery, fresh:				
8" long	1 stalk	7	0	50
diced	1 cup	20	0	151
diced, cooked	1 cup	21	0	132
Cereal:				
bran, added sugar	1 cup	144	0	493
bran flakes (40% bran)	1 cup	106	0	207
bran flakes with raisins	1 cup	144	0	212
corn flakes	1 cup	97	0	251
corn flakes, sugar-coated	1 cup	154	0	267
corn, puffed, presweetened	1 cup	114	0	255
corn, puffed, presweetened, cocoa-flavor	1 cup	117	0	228
corn, puffed, presweetened, fruit-flavor	1 cup	119	0	269
farina, instant, cooked	1 cup	135		461
farina, quick, cooked	1 cup	105	0	466
farina, regular, cooked	1 cup	103	0	353

FOOD	AMOUNT	CAL	CHOL (mg.)	SOD (mg.)
oat flakes, maple-flavored, cooked	1 cup	166	0	257
oat granules, maple-flavored, cooked	1 cup	147	0	176
oatmeal or rolled oats, dry	1 cup	312	0	2
oatmeal or rolled oats, cooked	1 cup	132	0	523
oats, shredded, sweetened	1 cup	171	0	275
rice, granulated, cooked	1 cup	123	0	431
rice, oven-popped	1 cup	117	0	283
rice, oven-popped, presweetened	1 cup	175	0	318
rice, puffed	1 cup	60	0	t
rice, puffed, presweetened	1 cup	140	0	148
rice, puffed, presweetened, cocoa-flavor	1 cup	140	0	148
wheat flakes	1 cup	106	0	310
wheat germ	1 Tbsp.	23	0	t
wheat, puffed	1 cup	54	0	1
wheat, puffed presweetened	1 cup	132	0	56
wheat, shredded	1 biscuit	89	0	1
wheat, shredded, spoon size	1 cup	177	0	2
wheat, whole meal, cooked	1 cup	110	0	519
wheat with malted barley, instant, cooked	1 cup	196	0	250
wheat with malted barley, quick, cooked	1 cup	159	0	176
Cervelat (see Sausage)				
Chard, Swiss, fresh, cooked	1 cup	26	0	125
Cheese:				
American, processed	1 oz.	106	27	406
American, processed	1 cu. in.	66	17	250
American, processed, shredded	1 cup	418	100	1,284
blue or roquefort	1 cup	497	117	2,490
blue or roquefort	1 oz.	104	24	510
brick	1 oz.	105	25	—
brick	1 cu. in.	64	16	96
brie	1 oz.	95	28	178
camembert, domestic	1 oz.	85	20	239

FOOD	AMOUNT	CAL	CHOL (mg.)	SOD (mg.)
cheddar, domestic . . . . 1 oz.		114	30	176
cheddar, domestic . . . . . . 1 cu. in.		68	17	120
cheddar, domestic, shredded . . 1 cup		455	119	701
colby . . . . 1 oz.		112	27	171
colby . . . . 1 cu. in.		68	16	104
cottage, creamed . . . . 1 cup		217	31	850
cottage, low-fat (2%) . . . . . . 1 cup		203	19	918
cottage, uncreamed . . . . . . 1 cup		123	10	421
cream . . . . 1 Tbsp.		52	16	35
cream, whipped . . . . 1 Tbsp.		37	10	25
edam . . . . 1 oz.		101	25	316
feta . . . . 1 oz.		75	25	316
gouda . . . . 1 oz.		101	32	232
limburger . . . . 1 oz.		93	26	227
mozzarella, part-skim . . . . . . 1 oz.		72	16	132
neufchatel . . . . 1 oz.		74	22	113
parmesan . . . . 1 oz.		111	19	454
parmesan, grated . . . . 1 cup		467	113	1,488
parmesan, grated . . . . . . 1 Tbsp.		23	4	93
provalone . . . . 1 oz.		100	20	248
ricotta, part-skim . . . . .1 cup		340	76	307
Swiss, domestic . . . . 1 oz.		107	26	74
Swiss, domestic . . . . 1 cu. in.		56	14	39
Swiss, processed . . . . 1 oz.		95	24	388
Swiss, processed . . . . 1 cu. in.		60	15	245
Cheese food, American, processed . . . . 1 Tbsp.		45	10	230
Cheese spread, American . . . . 1 Tbsp.		40	9	228
Cheese straws, 5" long 1		27	2	43
Cherimoya, fresh, 5" dia. 1/4		115	0	—
Cherries:				
candied 10		119	0	8
sour, canned, unsweetened . . . 1 cup		105	0	5
sour, fresh, whole, (pitted) . . . 1 cup		90	0	3
sweet, canned, sweetened . . . . 1 cup		208	0	3
sweet, canned, unsweetened . . 1 cup		119	0	2
sweet, fresh, whole (pitted) . . . 1 cup		102	0	3

FOOD	AMOUNT	CAL	CHOL (mg.)	SOD (mg.)
Chestnuts:				
in shell 10		141	0	4
shelled . . . . 1 cup		310	0	10
Chewing gum, sweetened . . . . . 1 stick		6	0	t
Chicken, lean, trimmed, cooked (no skin):				
broiler . . . . 4 oz.		154	93	75
fryer, dark meat, fried . . . . . 4 oz.		250	126	100
fryer, light meat, fried . . . . . 4 oz.		224	126	77
hen or cocks, chopped . . . . 1 cup		291	180	77
roaster, dark meat . . . . 4 oz.		209	93	100
roaster, light meat . . . . 4 oz.		207	93	75
roaster, light meat, chopped . . 1 cup		255	115	92
Chicken a la king, homemade . . . 1 cup		468	185	760
Chicken, canned, meat only . . . . 1 cup		406	155	850
Chicken pot pie, homemade, 9" dia. . . . . 1/3 pie		545	71	594
Chickpeas (Garbanzos), ... 1 cup		720	0	52
Chicory, fresh, chopped . . . . . 1 cup		14	0	6
Chili con carne, with beans, canned . . . . 1 cup		339	40	1,354
Chili sauce, tomato, bottled . . . 1 Tbsp.		16	0	201
Chives, fresh, chopped . . . . . . 1 Tbsp.		1	0	—
Chocolate, baking:				
bitter . . . . 1 oz.		143	40	1
semi-sweet, morsels or chips . . 1 cup		862	240	3
Chocolate, bittersweet or sweet (see Candy)				
Chocolate milk (see Milk)				
Chocolate syrup:				
thin type . . . . 2 Tbsp.		92	1	20
fudge topping . . . . 2 Tbsp.		124	t	33
Chop suey, with meat, homemade . . . . 1 cup		300	64	1,053
Chow mein, with meat, homemade . . . . 1 cup		255	77	718
Cider (see Apple, juice)				
Citron, candied . . . . 1 oz.		89	0	82

FOOD	AMOUNT	CAL	CHOL (mg.)	SOD (mg.)
Clams:				
canned, chopped or minced . .	1 cup	157	100	550
fresh, hard or round, raw	1 pint	363	388	930
fresh, soft, raw	1 pint	372	228	163
juice, bottled	1 cup	46	t	—
Cocoa:				
beverage powder	1 oz.	98	0	76
medium fat powder	1 Tbsp.	14	0	t
medium fat powder, with				
alkali	1 Tbsp.	14	0	39
Coconut:				
dried, unsweetened	1 oz.	188	0	94
fresh	2" sq.	156	0	10
fresh, shredded	1 cup	277	0	18
Coconut liquid:				
cream	1 Tbsp.	50	0	1
milk	1 cup	605	0	60
water	1 cup	53	0	60
Cod:				
canned, flaked	1 cup	119	—	—
dehydrated, shredded	1 cup	158	—	—
dried, salted	1 oz.	37	—	3,402
fresh, broiled with margarine .	4 oz.	192	65	124
Coffee, prepared, plain	1 cup	2	0	2
Cola (see Beverages)				
Cold cuts:				
bologna, all meat	1 oz.	79	20	292
bologna, with binders	1 oz.	74	19	290
braunschweiger (smoked				
liverwurst)	1 oz.	90	—	—
capicola	1 oz.	141	—	—
deviled ham, canned	1 Tbsp.	46	15	122
liverwurst, unsmoked	1 oz.	87	50	264
luncheon meat (see Luncheon meats)				
mortadella	1 oz.	89	—	—
salami	1 oz.	128	30	425
Coleslaw, commercial:				
with boiled dressing	1 cup	114	0	322

FOOD	AMOUNT	CAL	CHOL (mg.)	SOD (mg.)
with mayonnaise	1 cup	173	10	144
Collards:				
fresh, cooked	1 cup	63	0	40
frozen, chopped, cooked	1 cup	51	0	27
Cookies:				
animal crackers	10	112	t	79
brownie, from mix, 1-3/4" sq.	1	86	17	33
brownie, frozen, iced, 1-1/2"x1-3/4"	1	103	17	49
brownie, homemade, with nuts, 1-3/4" sq.	1	97	17	50
butter thins, 2" dia.	1	23	3	21
chocolate chips, commercial 2-1/4" dia.	1	50	10	42
chocolate chip, homemade, 2-1/3" dia.	1	51	15	35
coconut bars, 3x1-1/4"	1	45	10	13
fig bars, 1-5/8" sq.	1	50	t	35
gingersnaps, 2" dia.	1	29	10	40
graham crackers, chocolate coated	2" sq.	62	10	53
graham crackers, plain	2" sq.	28	t	48
graham crackers, sugar-honey	2" sq.	29	t	36
ladyfingers, 3-1/4" long	1	40	39	8
macaroons, 2-3/4"dia.	1	90	10	6
marshmallow, chocolate-coated, 2-1/8" dia.	1	53	10	27
marshmallow, coconut-coated, 2-1/8"dia.	1	74	10	38
molasses, 3-5/8" dia.	1	137	10	125
oatmeal, with raisins, 2-5/8" dia. . . .	1	58	10	21
peanut sandwich cookies, 1-3/4" dia.	1	58	10	22
peanut sugar wafers, 1-3/4"x1-3/8"	1	33	10	12
plain, 1-5/8" dia.	1	28	10	19
raisin, 2-1/4"x2"	1	54	t	8
sandwich-type, oval	1	74	15	73
sandwich-type, round	1	50	10	48

FOOD	AMOUNT	CAL	CHOL (mg.)	SOD (mg.)
sandwich-type, peanut (see Cookie, peanut)				
shortbread, 1-5/8" sq. 1		37	10	5
sugar, homemade, 2-1/4" dia. 1		36	10	25
sugar wafers, 2-1/2"x3/4" 1		17	10	7
vanilla wafers, 1-3/4" dia. 1		19	10	10
vanilla wafers, brown edge, 2-3/4" dia. 1		27	10	15
Cookie dough, plain, chilled, baked, 2-1/2" dia. 1		60	10	66
Corn:				
canned, cream style	1 cup	210	0	604
canned, kernels	1 cup	139	0	389
fresh, kernels, cooked	1 cup	137	0	t
fresh, on the cob, cooked	5" ear	70	0	t
frozen, kernels, cooked	1 cup	130	0	2
frozen, on the cob, cooked . . .	5" ear	118	0	1
Corn bread:				
from mix	2-1/2" sq.	178	38	263
homemade	2-1/2" sq.	186	58	491
Corn cereal (see Cereals)				
Corn flour (see Flour)				
Corn fritters, 2" dia. 1		132	t	167
Corn grits, degermed, cooked . . .	1 cup	125	0	502
Cornmeal:				
degermed, cooked	1 cup	120	0	264
degermed, dry	1 cup	502	0	1
whole, dry	1 cup	433	0	1
Corn muffins (see Muffins)				
Corn oil (see Oils)				
Corn pone, 9" dia.	3-1/2" arc	122	25	238
Corn pudding	1 cup	255	102	1,068
Cornstarch	1 Tbsp.	29	0	t
Cottonseed oil (see Oils)				
Cottage cheese (see Cheeses)				
Cottage pudding (see Cakes)				
Cowpeas (including blackeye peas)				

FOOD	AMOUNT	CAL	CHOL (mg.)	SOD (mg.)
canned	1 cup	179	0	602
fresh, cooked	1 cup	178	0	2
frozen, cooked	1 cup	221	0	66
Crab:				
canned, claw	1 cup	116	161	1,150
canned, white or king	1 cup	136	161	1,350
fresh, steamed	1 lb.	422	500	3,500
fresh, steamed, flaked	1 cup	116	125	1,700
fresh, steamed, pieces	1 cup	144	130	2,100
Cracker crumbs:				
butter	1 cup	366	t	874
graham	1 cup	326	t	570
soda	1 cup	307	0	770
Crackers:				
animal (see Cookies)				
butter, round 1-7/8" dia.	1	15	t	36
cheese, 1" sq.	10	52	t	112
graham (see Cookies)				
rye wafers, 3-1/2"x1-7/8"	1	22	0	57
saltines, 1-7/8" sq.	1	12	t	312
sandwich-type, cheese-peanut				
butter, 1-5/8" sq.	1	35	t	70
soda, 1-7/8" sq.	1	12	0	31
soda, biscuit, 2-3/8"x2-1/8"	1	22	0	55
soda, soup or oyster	1 cup	198	0	495
wheat thins	4	55	t	23
zwieback, 3-1/2"x1-1/2"	1	30	t	18
Cranberries, fresh, whole	1 cup	44	0	2
Cranberry juice cocktail, sweetened	1 cup	164	0	3
Cranberry-orange relish	1 cup	490	0	3
Cranberry sauce, canned, sweetened	1 cup	404	0	3
Cream:				
half and half	1 Tbsp.	20	6	6
light or table	1 Tbsp.	29	10	6
sour	1 Tbsp.	26	5	6
whipped(pressurized)	1 cup	154	46	78

FOOD	AMOUNT	CAL	CHOL (mg.)	SOD (mg.)
whipped, unsweetened . . . . . 1 cup		419	158	38
Whipping, heavy . . . . 1 Tbsp.		52	21	6
Cream puff, custard filling, 3-1/2" dia. 1		303	188	108
Cream substitute, non-dairy . . . 1 Tbsp.		20	0	12
Cress, garden, cooked . . . . . . 1 cup		31	0	11
Cucumbers:				
peeled, 6-3/8" long 1		22	0	9
peeled, sliced . . . . 1 cup		20	0	8
pickled (see Pickles)				
Cusk, steamed . . . . 1 oz.		30	–	21
Custard, baked . . . . 1 cup		305	278	209
Custard, frozen (see Ice cream)				

D

FOOD	AMOUNT	CAL	CHOL (mg.)	SOD (mg.)
Dandelion greens, cooked . . . . . 1 cup		35	0	46
Danish pastry, commercial 4-1/2" dia. 1		274	20	238
Dates, pitted:				
chopped . . . . 1 cup		488	0	2
whole 10		219	0	1
Deviled ham (see Cold cuts)				
Dewberries (see Blackberries)				
Doughnuts:				
cake-type, plain 3-5/8" dia. 1		227	30	291
yeast leavened, 3-3/4" dia. 1		176	30	99

E

FOOD	AMOUNT	CAL	CHOL (mg.)	SOD (mg.)
Eclair, custard filled, choc. frosted, 5" long 1		239	30	82
Egg, chicken, large:				
fried 1		99	285	155
hard cooked 1		82	274	61
omelet or scrambled 1		111	285	164
poached 1		82	274	136
raw, white 1		17	0	48

FOOD	AMOUNT	CAL	CHOL (mg.)	SOD (mg.)
raw, whole 1		82	274	61
raw, yolk 1		59	274	9
Eggnog	1 cup	342	149	138
Eggplant, fresh, cooked	1 cup	38	0	2
Egg substitute	1 cup	384	5	479
Endive, fresh, chopped	1 cup	10	0	7
Escarole (see Endive)				

F

FOOD	AMOUNT	CAL	CHOL (mg.)	SOD (mg.)
Farina (see Cereals)				
Fat, vegetable shortening	1 Tbsp.	111	0	0
Figs:				
canned, sweetened	1 cup	218	0	5
canned, unsweetened	1 cup	119	0	5
dried 1		55	0	7
fresh, 2-1/4" dia. 1		40	0	1
Filberts (hazelnuts):				
in shell 10		87	0	1
shelled, chopped	1 Tbsp.	44	0	1
shelled, whole	1 cup	856	0	3
Fish (see individual kinds)				
Fish cakes, frozen, breaded, fried, 3" dia. 1		103	40	428
Fish flakes, canned	1 cup	183	—	—
Fish sticks, frozen, breaded, cooked	1 oz. stick	50	15	20
Flounder, fresh, baked with margarine	4 oz.	228	65	268
Flour:				
all purpose, sifted	1 cup	419	0	2
bread, sifted	1 cup	420	0	2
buckwheat, dark, sifted	1 cup	326	0	4
buckwheat, light, sifted	1 cup	340	0	4
cake or pastry, sifted	1 cup	349	0	2
carob	1 cup	495	0	—
corn	1 cup	431	0	1
gluten (45%)	1 cup	510	0	3

FOOD	AMOUNT	CAL	CHOL (mg.)	SOD (mg.)
rye, dark, unsifted	1 cup	419	0	1
rye, light, unsifted	1 cup	364	0	1
soybean, defatted	1 cup	326	0	1
wheat, whole	1 cup	400	0	4
Frankfurters:				
all meat smoked, 4-3/4" long	1	124	48	499
all meat, unsmoked, 5" long	1	133	48	383
canned, 4-7/8" long	1	106	40	–
with binders, 5" long	1	112	38	399
Frostings (see Cake icings)				
Frozen custard (see Ice cream)				
Fruit cocktail:				
canned, sweetened	1 cup	194	0	13
canned, unsweetened	1 cup	91	0	12
Fruit salad:				
canned, sweetened	1 cup	191	0	3
canned, unsweetened	1 cup	86	0	2
G				
Garbanzos (see Chickpeas)				
Garlic, raw	1 clove	4	0	1
Gelatin:				
dry, 1/4 oz. envelope	1	23	0	0
dessert, prepared	1 cup	142	0	122
Gin (see Beverages)				
Ginger ale (see Beverages)				
Gingerbread (see Cake)				
Ginger root:				
candied	1 oz.	96	0	–
fresh	1 lb.	207	0	25
Gluten flour (see Flour)				
Goat Milk (see Milk)				
Goose, domesticated, cooked	3 oz.	198	36	105
Gooseberries, fresh	1 cup	59	0	2
Granadilla (passion fruit), fresh	1	16	0	5
Grapefruit:				
canned, sweetened	1 cup	178	0	3

FOOD	AMOUNT	CAL	CHOL (mg.)	SOD (mg.)
canned, unsweetened	1 cup	73	0	10
fresh, sections	1 cup	82	0	2
fresh, 3-9/16" dia.	1/2	40	0	1
juice, canned, sweetened	1 cup	133	0	3
juice, canned, unsweetened	1 cup	101	0	2
juice, fresh	1 cup	96	0	2
juice, frozen, sweetened	1 cup	117	0	2
juice, frozen, unsweetened	1 cup	101	0	2
Grapefruit-orange juice:				
canned, sweetened	1 cup	125	0	2
canned, unsweetened	1 cup	106	0	2
frozen, unsweetened	1 cup	109	0	t
Grapes:				
canned, sweetened	1 cup	197	0	10
canned, unsweetened	1 cup	125	0	10
fresh, American-type	1 cup	70	0	3
fresh, European-type	1 cup	107	0	5
juice, canned	1 cup	167	0	5
juice, frozen, sweetened	1 cup	133	0	3
Grape drink (30% grape juice)	1 cup	135	0	3
Grits (see Corn)				
Groundcherries, fresh	1 cup	74	0	—
Guava, fresh	1 med.	48	0	3
Gum (see Chewing Gum)				

H

FOOD	AMOUNT	CAL	CHOL (mg.)	SOD (mg.)
Haddock, fresh, oven-fried	4 oz.	188	77	200
Halibut, fresh, broiled with margarine	4 oz.	192	77	152
Ham (see Pork)				
Hamburger (see Beef)				
Hazelnuts (see Filberts)				
Hash (see Beef, corned)				
Headcheese (see Sausage)				
Heart, lean, cooked, chopped:				
beef	1 cup	273	398	151

FOOD	AMOUNT	CAL	CHOL (mg.)	SOD (mg.)
calf	1 cup	302	–	164
chicken	1 cup	268	350	192
hog	1 cup	283	–	94
lamb	1 cup	377	–	–
turkey	1 cup	257	327	79
Herring:				
canned, plain, 3-1/2" long	1	221	103	292
canned, tomato sauce, 4-3/4" long	1	97	–	–
pickled, 7" long	1	112	206	–
smoked, 7" long	1	137	206	3,513
Hominy grits (see Corn grits)				
Honey, strained or extracted	1 Tbsp.	64	0	1
Honeydew melon:				
fresh, 7" long	1/10	49	0	18
fresh, diced or balls	1 cup	56	0	20
frozen balls, sweetened	1 cup	143	0	21
Horseradish, prepared	1 Tbsp.	6	0	14
Hyacinth-beans, young pods, cuts	1 cup	32	0	2

I

Ice cream:				
plain, 10% fat	1 cup	269	59	116
plain, 16% fat	1 cup	349	88	108
soft serve (froz.en custard)	1 cup	377	153	153
Ice milk:				
plain, 5% fat	1 cup	184	18	105
soft serve	1 cup	223	13	163
Icings (see Cake icings)				

J

Jams and preserves, all flavors	1 Tbsp.	54	0	2
Jellies, all flavors	1 Tbsp.	49	0	3
Jerusalem artichokes (see Artichokes)				
Juices (see individual kinds)				

FOOD	AMOUNT	CAL	CHOL (mg.)	SOD (mg.)
K				
Kale:				
fresh, cooked	1 cup	43	0	47
frozen, cooked	1 cup	40	0	27
Kidney, beef, sliced, cooked	1 cup	353	1,125	354
Kippered herring (see Herring, smoked)				
Knockwurst (see Sausage)				
Kohlrabi, fresh, diced, cooked . . .	1 cup	40	0	10
Kumquat, fresh	1 sml.	15	0	5
L				
Ladyfingers (see Cookies)				
Lamb, lean, trimmed, cooked:				
leg	3 oz.	158	85	60
loin chops	4 oz.	213	110	78
rib chops	4 oz.	240	110	76
shoulder	3 oz.	174	85	56
shoulder, diced	1 cup	287	150	92
Lard	1 Tbsp.	117	12	0
Leeks (see Onions)				
Lemons:				
fresh, 2-1/8" dia.	1	20	0	1
juice, canned, unsweetened .	1 Tbsp.	3	0	t
juice, fresh	1 Tbsp.	4	0	t
juice, frozen, unsweetened . .	1 Tbsp.	3	0	t
Lemonade, frozen, sweetened . . .	1 cup	107	0	16
Lentils, dry, cooked	1 cup	212	0	16
Lettuce, raw:				
Boston or bibb, large leaf	1 leaf	2	0	1
Boston or bibb, shredded or				
chopped	1 cup	8	0	5
iceberg, wedge	1/4 head	18	0	12
iceberg, shredded or chopped .	1 cup	7	0	5
looseleaf, shredded or				
chopped	1 cup	10	0	5

FOOD	AMOUNT	CAL	CHOL (mg.)	SOD (mg.)
romaine, shredded or chopped	1 cup	10	0	5
Lima beans (see Beans, lima)				
Limes:				
fresh, 2" dia.	1	19	0	1
juice, canned, unsweetened .	1 Tbsp.	4	0	t
juice, fresh	1 Tbsp.	4	0	t
Limeade, frozen, sweetened	1 cup	102	0	t
Liver, cooked:				
beef (fried)	3 oz.	195	372	156
calf (fried)	3 oz.	222	372	100
chicken	4 oz.	187	853	69
chicken, chopped	1 cup	231	883	71
hog (fried)	3 oz.	205	372	94
lamb	4 oz.	296	496	97
turkey, chopped	1 cup	244	876	89
Liver paste (see Pate de foie gras)				
Liverwurst (see Sausage)				
Lobster fresh or canned:				
cooked	1 lb.	431	161	953
cooked, chopped	1 cup	138	123	305
Lobster Newberg	1 cup	485	456	573
Lobster paste, canned	1 tsp.	13	—	—
Loganberries, fresh	1 cup	89	0	1
Luncheon meat, canned or packaged:				
boiled ham	1 oz.	66	70	49
pork, chopped	1 oz.	83	—	350
Lychees, fresh	10	58	0	3

M

Macaroni, cooked:				
cold	1 cup	117	0	1
hot	1 cup	155	0	1
Macaroni and cheese;				
canned	1 cup	228	21	730
homemade	1 cup	430	21	1,086

FOOD	AMOUNT	CAL	CHOL (mg.)	SOD (mg.)
Mackerel:				
Atlantic, fresh, broiled with margarine	4 oz.	268	80	130
Pacific, canned	3 oz.	153	80	—
salted	1 oz.	86	27	—
Malt, dry	1 oz.	104	t	75
Malt extract, dried	1 oz.	104	t	23
Mandarin oranges (see Tangerines)				
Mangos, fresh:				
diced	1 cup	109	0	12
whole	1	152	0	16
Margarine:				
regular	1 stick	816	*	1,119
regular or soft	1 Tbsp.	102	*	140
regular	1 pat	36	*	49
whipped	1 Tbsp.	68	*	93
Varies, depending on type; can equal zero.				
Marmalade, citrus	1 Tbsp.	51	0	3
Matai (see Waterchestnuts)				
Mayonnaise (see Salad dressings)				
Meat (see individual kinds)				
Melons (see individual kinds)				
Milk, cows:				
buttermilk	1 cup	99	9	257
chocolate, hot	1 cup	218	33	123
chocolate-flavored, low-fat	1 cup	179	17	150
chocolate-flavored, whole	1 cup	208	30	149
condensed, sweetened	1 cup	982	104	389
dried, non-fat, instant	1 cup	244	12	373
evaporated, canned	1 cup	338	74	266
low-fat, 2%	1 cup	121	18	122
skim	1 cup	86	4	126
whole	1 cup	157	35	119
Milk, goat's, whole	1 cup	168	28	122
Milk, malted, powder	1 oz.	116	t	55
Mixed vegetables (see Vegetables, mixed)				

FOOD	AMOUNT	CAL	CHOL (mg.)	SOD (mg.)
Mollases, cane:				
light	1 Tbsp.	50	0	3
blackshop	1 Tbsp.	43	0	19
Mortadella (see Cold cuts)				
Muffins:				
from mix, corn 2-3/8" dia.	1	130	21	192
homemade, blueberry, 2-3/8" dia. . .	1	112	21	253
homemade, bran, 2-5/8" dia.	1	104	21	179
homemade, corn, 2-3/8" dia.	1	126	21	192
homemade, plain, 3" dia.	1	118	21	176
Mushrooms:				
canned, chopped or sliced . . .	1 cup	42	0	800
fresh, chopped or sliced	1 cup	20	0	10
Muskmelons (see individual kinds)				
Mustard greens:				
fresh, cooked	1 cup	32	0	25
frozen, chopped, cooked	1 cup	30	0	15
Mustard spinach, fresh, cooked . .	1 cup	29	0	–
Mustard, prepared:				
brown	1 tsp.	5	0	65
yellow	1 tsp.	4	0	63
Mussels:				
canned	4 oz.	129	–	–
fresh	4 oz.	108	–	–

N

FOOD	AMOUNT	CAL	CHOL (mg.)	SOD (mg.)
Nectarines, fresh, 2-1/2" dia.	1	88	0	8
Noodles:				
chowmein, canned	1 cup	220	5	–
egg, cooked	1 cup	200	50	3
Nuts (see individual kinds)				

O

FOOD	AMOUNT	CAL	CHOL (mg.)	SOD (mg.)
Oats, oatmeal (see Cereal)				
Oil:				
Cooking or salad*	1 Tbsp.	120	0	0

*corn, cottonseed, safflower, sesame, soybean oils, and soybean-cottonseed oil blend

FOOD	AMOUNT	CAL	CHOL (mg.)	SOD (mg.)
olive	1 Tbsp.	119	0	0
peanut	1 Tbsp.	119	0	0
Okra:				
fresh, sliced	1 cup	36	0	3
fresh, sliced, cooked	1 cup	46	0	3
frozen, sliced, cooked	1 cup	70	0	4
Oleomargarine (see Margarine)				
Olive oil (see Oil)				
Olives, pickled, canned or bottled:				
green, large, 3/4" dia.	10	45	0	926
green, small, 5/8" dia.	10	33	0	686
ripe, ascolano, 3/4" dia.	10	61	0	385
ripe, ascolano, sliced	1 cup	174	0	1,098
Olives, ripe:				
manzanillo, 3/4" dia.	10	61	0	385
Manzanillo, sliced	1 cup	174	0	1,098
mission, 3/4" dia.	10	87	0	355
mission, sliced	1 cup	248	0	1,013
salt'n oil (Greek style)	10	65	0	631
sevillano, 1" dia.	10	95	0	847
Onions:				
dehydrated	1 Tbsp.	18	0	6
green, bulb and top, chopped	1 Tbsp.	2	0	t
green, bulb and white, chopped	1 Tbsp.	3	0	t
green, tops only, chopped (scallions)	1 Tbsp.	2	0	t
mature, chopped	1 cup	65	0	17
mature, whole or sliced, cooked	1 cup	61	0	15
Oranges, fresh:				
Florida, 2-5/8" dia.	1	66	0	1
naval, 2-7/8" dia.	1	71	0	1
Valencia, 2-5/8" dia.	1	62	0	1
sections	1 cup	88	0	2

FOOD	AMOUNT	CAL	CHOL (mg.)	SOD (mg.)
Orange Juice:				
canned, sweetened	1 cup	130	0	2
canned, unsweetened	1 cup	120	0	2
fresh	1 cup	112	0	2
frozen, unsweetened	1 cup	114	0	2
Orange-cranberry relish (see cranberry-orange relish)				
Orange-grapefruit juice (see grapefruit-orange juice)				
Orange peel, candied	1 oz.	90	0	—
Oysters, raw, meat only:				
Eastern, 13-19 med.	1 cup	158	120	175
Pacific and Western, 4-6 med.	1 cup	218	120	—
Oysters, fried, 2-3 med.	1 oz.	68	60	58
Oyster stew, homemade	1 cup	233	63	814

P

FOOD	AMOUNT	CAL	CHOL (mg.)	SOD (mg.)
Pancakes:				
from mix, buckwheat, 6" dia.	1	146	54	339
from mix, buckwheat, 4" dia.	1	54	21	125
from mix, plain & buttermilk, 6" dia.	1	164	54	412
from mix, plain & buttermilk, 4" dia.	1	61	21	152
homemade, 6" dia.	1	169	54	310
homemade, 4" dia.	1	62	21	115
Papaws, fresh, 2" dia.	1	83	0	—
Papayas:				
fresh, 3-1/2" dia.	1	119	0	9
fresh, cubed	1 cup	55	0	4
Parsley, fresh:				
chopped	1 Tbsp	2	0	2
whole sprigs	10	4	0	5
Parsnips, cooked:				
diced	1 cup	102	0	12
mashed	1 cup	139	0	17
whole, 6" long	1	23	0	3
Passion fruit (see Granadilla)				
Pastina, egg, dry	1 cup	651	—	9

FOOD	AMOUNT	CAL	CHOL (mg.)	SOD (mg.)
Pastry shell (see Pie crust)				
Pate de foie gras, canned	1 Tbsp.	60	45	105
Peaches:				
canned, sweetened	1 cup	200	0	5
canned, unsweetened	1 cup	76	0	5
dehydrated, uncooked	1 cup	340	0	21
dried halves, uncooked	10 med.	341	0	21
fresh, 2-1/2" dia.	1	38	0	1
fresh, diced	1 cup	70	0	2
frozen, sweetened, sliced	1 cup	220	0	5
nectar, canned (40% fruit) . . .	1 cup	120	0	2
Peanut butter, commercial . . .	1 Tbsp.	94	t	97
Peanuts, roasted:				
in shell, jumbo	10	105	0	1
shelled, chopped	1 Tbsp.	52	0	t
shelled, salted, chopped or				
whole	1 cup	842	0	602
shelled, salted, Spanish	20	53	0	38
shelled, salted Virginia	10	53	0	38
Peanut oil (see Oils)				
Pears:				
canned, sweetened	1 cup	194	0	3
canned, unsweetened	1 cup	78	0	2
dried halves, uncooked	10	469	0	12
fresh, Bartlett, 2-1/2" dia.	1	100	0	3
fresh, Bosc, 2-1/2" dia.	1	86	0	3
fresh, D'Anjou, 3" dia.	1	122	0	4
fresh, sliced or cubed	1 cup	101	0	3
nectar, canned (40% fruit) . . .	1 cup	130	0	3
Peas:				
blackeye (see Cowpeas)				
green, canned, early or June . .	1 cup	150	0	401
green, canned, sweet	1 cup	136	0	401
green, fresh	1 cup	122	0	3
green, fresh, cooked	1 cup	114	0	2
green, froz.en, cooked	1 cup	109	0	184
split, cooked	1 cup	230	0	26
Peas and carrots, froz.en, cooked .	1 cup	85	0	134

FOOD	AMOUNT	CAL	CHOL (mg.)	SOD (mg.)
Pecans:				
in shell, large (64-77/lb.) 10		236	0	t
shelled, chopped . . . . 1 Tbsp.		52	0	t
shelled, halves . . . . 1 cup		742	0	t
Peppers:				
hot, green, canned . . . . . . 1 cup		49	0	—
hot, red, canned . . . . 1 cup		51	0	—
sweet green, 3" dia. . . . . 1 ring		2	0	1
sweet green, sliced . . . . . . 1 cup		18	0	10
sweet green, sliced, cooked . . . 1 cup		24	0	12
sweet red, 3" dia. . . . . 1 ring		3	0	t
sweet red, sliced . . . . 1 cup		25	0	10
Perch:				
fresh, cooked . . . . 4 oz.		130	85	77
ocean (redfish), fresh . . . . . . 4 oz.		100	85	—
Persimmons, fresh:				
Japanese or kaki, 2-1/2" dia. 1		129	0	10
native 1		31	0	t
Pickles, cucumber:				
"bread and butter," slices, 1/4" thick . 2		11	0	101
dill, slices, 1/4" thick 2		1	0	186
dill, spear, 6" long 1		3	0	428
dill, whole, 4" long 1		15	0	1,929
sour, whole, 4" long 1		14	0	1,827
sweet, chopped . . . . 1 Tbsp.		15	0	69
sweet, gherkin, 3" long 1		51	0	252
sweet, gherkin, midget 1		9	0	48
sweet, spear, 4-1/2" long 1		29	0	148
Pickles, mustard (chow-chow):				
sour . . . . 1 Tbsp.		70	0	3,211
sweet . . . . 1 Tbsp.		18	0	81
Pickle relish, sweet . . . . 1 Tbsp.		21	0	107
Pie:				
apple, frozen, baked, 8" dia. . . . . 4-1/8" arc		231	120	195
apple, homemade, 9" dia. . . . 3-1/2" arc		302	120	355
banana custard, homemade, 9" dia. . . . . 3-1/2" arc		252	140	221

FOOD	AMOUNT	CAL	CHOL (mg.)	SOD (mg.)
blackberry, homemade, 9" dia.	3-1/2" arc	287	70	316
blueberry, homemade, 9" dia.	3-1/2" arc	286	70	316
Boston cream (see Cake)				
cherry, frozen, baked 8" dia.	4-1/8" arc	282	70	222
cherry, homemade, 9" dia. .	3-1/2" arc	308	70	359
chocolate chiffon, homemade 9" dia.	3-1/2" arc	266	137	204
coconut custard, from mix, 8" dia.	4-1/8" arc	270	120	313
coconut custard, frozen, baked, 8" dia.	4-1/8" arc	249	120	252
coconut custard, homemade, 9" dia.	3-1/2" arc	268	120	282
custard, homemade, 9" dia.	3-1/2" arc	249	120	327
lemon meringue, homemade, 9" dia.	3-1/8" arc	268	98	296
mince, homemade, 9" dia. .	3-1/2" arc	320	70	529
peach, homemade, 9" dia. .	3-1/2" arc	301	70	316
pecan, homemade, 9" dia. .	3-1/2" arc	431	70	228
pineapple, homemade, 9" dia.	3-1/2" arc	299	70	320
pumpkin, homemade, 9" dia.	3-1/2" arc	241	70	244
rhubarb, homemade, 9" dia.	3-1/2" arc	299	70	319
strawberry, homemade, 9" dia.	3-1/2" arc	184	70	180
sweet potato, homemade, 9" dia.	3-1/2" arc	243	t	249
Piecrust or plain pastry" baked, 9" dia.	1 shell	900	t	1,100
from mix, 10 oz. pkg., baked . .	1 shell	1,485	t	2,602
Pignolias (see Pinenuts)				
Pigs' feet, pickled	2 oz.	113	335	—
Pimentoes, canned, with liquid . . .	2 oz.	15	0	—

FOOD	AMOUNT	CAL	CHOL (mg.)	SOD (mg.)
Pineapple:				
canned, sweetened, cuts*	1 cup	189	0	3
canned, sweetened, sliced,				
3" dia.	1 ring	43	0	1
canned, unsweetened, cuts* . .	1 cup	96	0	2
*chunk, crushed, tidbits				
Pineapple:				
fresh, diced	1 cup	81	0	2
fresh, sliced, 3-1/2" dia.	1	44	0	1
frozen, sweetened, chunks . . .	1 cup	208	0	5
juice, canned, unsweetened . .	1 cup	138	0	3
juice, frozen, unsweetened . . .	1 cup	130	0	3
Pineapple, candied	1 oz.	90	0	13
Pineapple and grapefruit juice drink,				
canned (50% fruit juices) . . .	1 cup	135	0	t
Pineapple and orange juice drink,				
canned (40% fruit juice) . . .	1 cup	135	0	t
Pinenuts:				
pignolias, shelled	1 oz.	156	0	—
pinons, shelled	1 oz.	180	0	—
Pistachio nuts, shelled	1 oz.	168	0	—
Pitanga, fresh, pitted	1 cup	87	0	—
Pizza:				
frozen, baked, 10" dia.	4-1/2" arc	139	15	367
frozen, baked, 5-1/4" dia . . .	1 pizza	179	15	472
homemade, 14" dia.	5-1/3" arc	153	16	456
Plantain (baking bananas), fresh,				
11" long	1	313	0	13
Plums:				
canned, sweetened	1 cup	214	0	3
canned, unsweetened	1 cup	114	0	5
fresh, Damson, 1" dia.	10	66	0	2
fresh, Damson, halves	1 cup	112	0	3
fresh, Japanese, 2-1/8" dia.	1	32	0	1
fresh, Japanese, diced	1 cup	79	0	2
fresh, prune-type, 1-1/2" dia.	1	21	0	t
fresh, prune-type, halves	1 cup	124	0	2
Poha (see Groundcherries)				

FOOD	AMOUNT	CAL	CHOL (mg.)	SOD (mg.)
Pokeberry shoots, cooked . . . . . 1 cup		33	0	–
Pollock, fresh creamed . . . . . . 1 cup		320	–	278
Pomegranate, fresh, 3-3/8" dia. 1		97	0	5
Popcorn, popped:				
plain . . . . 1 cup		23	0	t
salt and oil added . . . . 1 cup		41	0	175
sugar-coated . . . . 1 cup		134	0	t
Popovers, homemade, 4" high 1		90	59	88
Pork, lean, trimmed, cooked:				
ham, cured . . . . 3 oz.		159	80	770
ham, cured, canned . . . . 4 oz.		214	105	1,062
ham, fresh . . . . 3 oz.		184	80	62
ham, fresh, diced . . . . 1 cup		304	160	102
ham, fresh, ground . . . . . . 1 cup		239	120	80
loin chops, fresh . . . . 3 oz.		226	75	64
loin roast, fresh . . . . 3 oz.		216	75	61
shoulder, Boston butt, cured . . 3 oz.		207	75	845
shoulder, Boston butt, fresh . . 3 oz.		207	75	56
shoulder, picnic, cured . . . . . 3 oz.		179	75	863
shoulder, picnic, fresh . . . . . 3 oz.		180	75	43
spareribs (with fat) . . . . 4 oz.		499	80	41
Pork sausage (see Bacon)				
Potato, sweet:				
baked in skin, 4-3/4" long 1		161	0	14
boiled in skin, 4-3/4" long 1		172	0	15
boiled in skin, mashed . . . . 1 cup		291	0	26
candied in syrup, 2-1/2" long 1		176	0	44
canned, chopped . . . . 1 cup		216	0	96
Potato, white:				
baked in skin, 4-3/4" long 1		145	0	6
boiled, in skin, 2-1/2" dia. 1		104	0	4
boiled, peeled, 2-1/2" dia. 1		73	0	2
boiled, peeled, diced or sliced . 1 cup		101	0	3
dehydrated flakes, prepared . . 1 cup		195	0	485
dehydrated granules, prepared 1 cup		202	0	538
French fried, 2-3-1/2" long 10		137	0	3
French fried, 1-2" long 10		96	0	2

FOOD	AMOUNT	CAL	CHOL (mg.)	SOD (mg.)
French fried, froz.en, oven-heated, 2-3-1/2"	10	110	0	2
French fried, froz.en, oven-heated, 1-2"	10	77	0	1
fried	1 cup	456	0	379
hash brown, cooked	1 cup	355	0	446
mashed, with milk	1 cup	137	4	632
scalloped	1 cup	255	14	870
Potato chips	10	114	t	200
Potato salad:				
with cooked salad dressing	1 cup	248	t	1,320
with mayonnaise and eggs	1 cup	363	162	1,200
Potato sticks	1 cup	190	t	284
Pretzels:				
logs, 3" long	10	195	0	840
rods, 7-1/2" long	1	55	0	235
sticks, 3-1/8" long	10	23	0	101
sticks, 2-1/4" long	10	12	0	50
twisted, 3-ring	10	117	0	504
twisted, 1-ring	10	78	0	336
twisted, Dutch	1	62	0	269
twisted, thins	10	234	0	1,008
Prunes:				
dehydrated, uncooked	1 cup	344	0	11
dried, chopped	1 cup	408	0	13
dried, large	1	22	0	t
dried, medium	1	16	0	t
juice, canned or bottled	1 cup	197	0	5
Prune whip, baked	1 cup	140	40	148
Pudding:				
from mix, chocolate	1 cup	322	30	335
from mix, instant, chocolate	1 cup	325	30	322
homemade, chocolate	1 cup	385	38	146
homemade, vanilla	1 cup	283	35	166
Pumpkin, canned	1 cup	81	0	5
Pumpkin seeds, hulled	1 cup	774	0	—

FOOD	AMOUNT	CAL	CHOL (mg.)	SOD (mg.)
Q				
Quail, fresh, cooked	4 oz.	190	75	45
Quince, fresh	4 oz.	65	0	4
R				
Rabbit, domesticated, cooked, chopped	1 cup	302	127	57
Radishes, fresh:				
large	10	14	0	15
sliced	1 cup	20	0	21
Raisins, seedless:				
chopped	1 cup	390	0	36
whole	1 cup	419	0	39
whole	1 Tbsp.	26	0	2
Raspberries:				
fresh, black	1 cup	98	0	1
fresh, red	1 cup	70	0	1
frozen, red, sweetened	1 cup	245	0	3
Redfish (see Perch)				
Rhubarb:				
fresh, diced	1 cup	20	0	2
fresh, sweetened, cooked	1 cup	381	0	5
frozen, sweetened, cooked . . .	1 cup	386	0	8
Rice, cooked:				
brown, long grain	1 cup	232	0	550
white, long grain	1 cup	223	0	767
white, long grain, parboiled . .	1 cup	186	0	627
white, long grain, pre-cooked (instant)	1 cup	180	0	450
Rice cereal (see Cereal)				
Rice polish	1 cup	278	0	t
Rice pudding, with raisins	1 cup	387	30	188
Rockfish, fresh, cooked	4 oz.	120	65	96
Roe, herring, canned	4 oz.	134	404	—

FOOD	AMOUNT	CAL	CHOL (mg.)	SOD (mg.)
Rolls and buns, commercial, ready-to-serve:				
cloverleaf or dinner, 2" high 1		83	t	142
frankfurter or hamburger 1		119	t	202
hard roll, 3-3/4" dia. 1		156	t	313
hoagie or submarine, 11-1/2" long 1		392	t	783
Romaine (see Lettuce)				
Root beer (see Beverages)				
Rum (see Beverages)				
Rusk, 3-3/8" dia. 1		38	t	22
Rutabagas, fresh, cooked:				
cubed	1 cup	60	0	7
mashed	1 cup	84	0	10
Rye flour (see Flour)				
Rye wafers (see Crackers)				

S

FOOD	AMOUNT	CAL	CHOL (mg.)	SOD (mg.)
Safflower oil (see Oils)				
Salad dressings, commercial:				
blue cheese or roquefort . . .	1 Tbsp.	76	t	164
blue cheese or roquefort, low-calorie	1 Tbsp.	12	0	177
French	1 Tbsp.	66	t	219
French low-calorie	1 Tbsp.	15	0	126
Italian	1 Tbsp.	83	0	314
Italian, low-calorie	1 Tbsp.	8	0	t
mayonnaise	1 Tbsp.	101	10	84
Russian	1 Tbsp.	74	10	130
Russian, low-calorie	1 Tbsp.	23	1	26
salad dressing (mayonnaise-type)	1 Tbsp.	65	4	88
salad dressing, low calorie . .	1 Tbsp.	22	t	19
thousand island	1 Tbsp.	80	10	112
thousand island, low calorie .	1 Tbsp.	27	2	105
Salad dressing, homemade, cooked	1 Tbsp.	26	12	116
Salad oil (see Oils)				

FOOD	AMOUNT	CAL	CHOL (mg.)	SOD (mg.)
Salami (see Cold cuts)				
Salmon, canned:				
Atlantic	1 cup	447	80	—
chinook (king)	1 cup	462	80	—
*chum	1 cup	306	80	110
* No salt added				
coho (silver)	1 cup	337	80	772
pink (humpback)	1 cup	310	80	85
sockeye (red)	1 cup	376	80	1,148
Salmon, fresh:				
broiled with margarine	4 oz.	208	60	132
smoked	4 oz.	200	60	—
Salsify, fresh, cubed, cooked	1 cup	94	0	—
Salt, table:				
	1 cup	0	0	112,398
	1 Tbsp.	0	0	6,589
	1 tsp.	0	0	2,132
Sardines, Atlantic, canned, 3" long	1	24	25	99
Sauces, (see individual kinds)				
Sauerkraut, canned	1 cup	42	0	1,755
Sausage:				
blood (blood pudding)	1 oz.	112	—	—
bockwurst	1 link	172	—	—
brown-and-serve, cooked	1 link	72	10	—
cervelat	1 oz.	128	29	—
country-style	1 oz.	98	—	—
headcheese	1 oz.	76	65	—
knockwurst	1 ink	189	65	650
Polish, 5-3/8" long	1 link	231	75	450
pork, canned	1 link	46	10	—
pork, fresh, cooked	1 link	62	10	125
scrapple	1 oz.	61	—	—
souse	1 oz.	51	—	—
summer (thuringer cervelat)	1 oz.	87	29	—
Vienna, canned, 2" long	1 link	38	16	—
Scallions (see Onions)				
Scallops:				
bay and sea, fresh, cooked	4 oz.	127	60	301

FOOD	AMOUNT	CAL	CHOL (mg.)	SOD (mg.)
bay and sea, frozen, breaded, fried, reheated . . . . 4 oz.		220	61	330
Scrapple (see Sausage)				
Sesame oil (see Oils)				
Sesame seeds, dry, hulled . . . . 1 Tbsp.		47	0	4
Shad, fresh, baked . . . . 4 oz.		228	75	88
Shallot, bulbs, fresh, chopped . . 1 Tbsp.		7	0	1
Sherbet, orange . . . . 1 cup		270	14	88
Shortbread (see Cookies)				
Shrimp:				
canned (22-76) . . . . 1 cup		148	192	—
fresh, meat only 2-1/2" long 10		37	110	50
fried . . . . 4 oz.		256	250	212
Shrimp paste, canned . . . . .1 tsp.		13	—	—
Smelt, fresh . . . . 7 med.		100	77	30
Snails, raw, meat only . . . . 4 oz.		100	80	—
Soft drinks (see Beverages)				
Sole, fresh, cooked . . . . 4 oz.		90	77	89
Soup, canned, condensed:				
asparagus, cream of, prepared with milk . . . . . . 1 cup		147	15	1,068
asparagus, cream of, prepared with water . . . . . 1 cup		65	t	984
bean with pork, prepared with water . . . . . 1 cup		355	15	2,136
beef broth or consomme, prepared with water . . . . . 1 cup		31	t	782
beef noodle, prepared with water . . . . . 1 cup		67	t	917
celery, cream of, prepared with milk . . . . . . 1 cup		169	15	1,039
celery, cream of, prepared with water . . . . . 1 cup		86	t	955
chicken, consomme, prepared with water . . . . . 1 cup		22	t	722
chicken, cream of, prepared with milk . . . . . . 1 cup		179	15	1,054

FOOD	AMOUNT	CAL	CHOL (mg.)	SOD (mg.)
chicken, cream of,				
prepared with water	1 cup	94	t	970
chicken gumbo,				
prepared with water	1 cup	55	t	950
chicken noodle,				
prepared with water	1 cup	62	t	979
chicken vegetable,				
prepared with water	1 cup	76	t	1,034
chicken with rice,				
prepared with water	1 cup	48	t	917
clam chowder (Manhattan type),				
prepared with water	1 cup	81	t	938
minestrone,				
prepared with water	1 cup	105	0	995
mushroom, cream of,				
prepared with milk	1 cup	216	15	1,039
mushroom, cream of,				
prepared with water	1 cup	134	t	955
onion, prepared with water . . .	1 cup	65	t	1,051
pea, green,				
prepared with water	1 cup	130	t	899
pea, split,				
prepared with water	1 cup	145	t	941
tomato, prepared with milk . .	1 cup	173	15	1,055
tomato, prepared with water . .	1 cup	88	t	970
turkey noodle, prepared				
with water	1 cup	79	t	998
vegetable beef, prepared				
with water	1 cup	78	t	1,046
vegetable with beef broth,				
prepared with water	1 cup	78	t	845
vegetarian vegetable,				
prepared with water	1 cup	78	0	838
Soup, dehydrated, prepared according to package:				
beef noodle	1 cup	67	t	420
chicken noodle	1 cup	53	t	578
chicken with rice	1 cup	48	t	622
onion	1 cup	36	t	689
pea, green	1 cup	123	t	796

FOOD	AMOUNT	CAL	CHOL (mg.)	SOD (mg.)
Sour cream (see Cream)				
Soursop, raw, pureed	1 cup	146	0	32
Souse (see Sausages)				
Soybeans:				
curd (tofu) 2-1/2"x2-3/4"	1 piece	86	0	8
dry, cooked	1 cup	234	0	4
flour (see Flour)				
oil (see Oil)				
sprouts	1 cup	48	0	3
sprouts, cooked	1 cup	48	0	3
Soy sauce	1 Tbsp.	12	0	1,319
Spaghetti:				
canned, in tomato sauce, cheese . . .	1 cup	190	50	955
canned, with meatballs and sauce	1 cup	258	39	1,220
plain, cooked, "al dente"	1 cup	192	0	1
plain, cooked, tender stage . . .	1 cup	155	0	1
with homemade tomato sauce, cheese	1 cup	260	50	955
Spanish rice, homemade	1 cup	213	t	744
Spinach:				
canned	1 cup	49	0	484
fresh, chopped	1 cup	14	0	39
fresh, cooked	1 cup	41	0	90
frozen, chopped, cooked	1 cup	47	0	107
frozen, leaf, cooked	1 cup	46	0	93
Spot, fresh, baked	4 oz.	336	—	352
Squash, summer, fresh	1 cup	25	0	1
Squash, summer, cooked, sliced:				
crookneck or straightneck . . .	1 cup	27	0	2
scallop varieties	1 cup	29	0	2
zucchini or Italian	1 cup	22	0	2
Squash, winter, fresh:				
acorn, baked, 4" diam.	1/2	86	0	2
butternut, baked, mashed . . .	1 cup	139	0	2
butternut, boiled, mashed . . .	1 cup	100	0	2
hubbard, baked, mashed	1 cup	103	0	2

FOOD	AMOUNT	CAL	CHOL (mg.)	SOD (mg.)
hubbard, boiled, diced	1 cup	71	0	2
hubbard, boiled, mashed	1 cup	74	0	2
Squash, winter, frozen, cooked . .	1 cup	91	0	2
Starch, (see Cornstarch)				
Strawberries:				
fresh, whole	1 cup	55	0	1
frozen, sweetened, sliced	1 cup	278	0	3
frozen, sweetened, whole	1 cup	235	0	3
Sturgeon:				
fresh, cooked	4 oz.	180	80	124
smoked	4 oz.	168	80	222
Succotash, frozen, cooked	1 cup	158	0	65
Sugar, beet or cane:				
brown, packed	1 cup	821	0	66
granulated	1 cup	770	0	2
granulated	1 tsp.	15	0	t
granulated	1 packet	23	0	t
powdered, sifted	1 cup	385	0	1
powdered, unsifted	1 cup	462	0	1
Sugar, maple	1 oz.	99	0	4
Sunflower seeds, hulled	1 cup	812	0	44
Surinam cherry (see Pitanga)				
Sweet potatoes (see Potato, sweet)				
Swiss chard (see Chard, Swiss)				
Sword fish, fresh, broiled with margarine	4 oz.	184	77	—
Syrup:				
chocolate (see Chocolate syrup)				
corn, light or dark	1 cup	951	0	223
corn, light or dark	1 Tbsp.	59	0	14
maple	1 Tbsp.	50	0	2
sorghum	1 cup	848	0	96
sorghum	1 Tbsp.	53	0	6
table blend (cane and maple)	1 Tbsp.	50	0	t

FOOD	AMOUNT	CAL	CHOL (mg.)	SOD (mg.)
T				
Tangelo:				
fresh, 2-3/4" dia. 1		47	0	2
juice, fresh	1 cup	101	0	2
Tangerine, fresh:				
2-1/2" dia. 1		46	0	2
sections	1 cup	90	0	4
juice, canned, sweetened	1 cup	125	0	2
juice, canned unsweetened . . .	1 cup	106	0	2
juice, fresh	1 cup	106	0	2
juice, frozen, unsweetened . . .	1 cup	114	0	2
Tapioca:				
dried	1 cup	535	0	5
pudding	1 cup	221	159	257
Tartar sauce	1 Tbsp.	74	7	99
Thuringer (see Sausage)				
Tilefish, fresh, baked	4 oz.	156	–	–
Tomatoes:				
canned	1 cup	51	0	313
fresh, 2-3/5" dia. 1		27	0	4
fresh, cooked	1 cup	63	0	10
juice, canned or bottled	1 cup	46	0	486
juice cocktail, canned or bottled	1 cup	51	0	486
Tomato catsup (see Catsup)				
Tomato chili sauce (see Chili sauce)				
Tomato paste, canned	1 cup	215	0	100
Tomato puree, canned	1 lb.	177	0	1,810
Tongue cooked:				
beef	2 oz.	138	66	35
calf	2 oz.	91	–	–
hog	2 oz.	144	–	–
lamb	2 oz.	144	70	–
sheep	2 oz.	183	–	–
Tripe, canned	4 oz.	113	200	82
Trout, fresh, cooked	4 oz.	225	140	70

FOOD	AMOUNT	CAL	CHOL (mg.)	SOD (mg.)
Tuna:				
canned in oil	1 cup	315	102	—
canned in water	4 oz.	144	72	46
fresh, cooked	3 oz.	105	60	46
salad	1 cup	349	150	1,600
Turkey:				
canned, meat only	1 cup	414	—	844
cooked, chopped	1 cup	266	120	182
cooked, dark meat	3 oz.	173	86	84
cooked, light meat	3 oz.	150	65	70
Turkey giblets, cooked, chopped	1 cup	338	175	110
Turkey pot pie, homemade, 9" dia.	1/3 pie	550	71	663
Turnip, cooked:				
cubed	1 cup	36	0	53
mashed	1 cup	53	0	78
Turnip greens:				
canned	1 cup	42	0	548
fresh, cooked	1 cup	29	0	—
frozen, chopped, cooked	1 cup	38	0	28

V

FOOD	AMOUNT	CAL	CHOL (mg.)	SOD (mg.)
Veal, lean, trimmed cooked:				
chuck and stew cuts	3 oz.	200	84	41
chuck and stew cuts, diced	1 cup	329	138	68
loin cuts	3 oz.	199	84	55
plate, breast	4 oz.	344	112	52
rib roast	3 oz.	229	84	57
rib roast, ground	1 cup	296	109	73
round with rump	3 oz.	184	84	56
Vegetable juice cocktail, canned	1 cup	41	0	484
Vegetables, mixed, frozen, cooked	1 cup	116	0	96
Venison, lean, uncooked	3 oz.	107	—	—
Vienna sausage (see Sausages)				
Vinegar:				
cider	1 Tbsp.	2	0	t
distilled	1 Tbsp.	2	0	t

FOOD	AMOUNT	CAL	CHOL (mg.)	SOD (mg.)
Vodka (see Beverages)				

W

FOOD	AMOUNT	CAL	CHOL (mg.)	SOD (mg.)
Waffles:				
from mix, round, 7" dia. 1		206	90	515
from mix, square, 4-1/2"x4-1/2" 1		138	60	343
frozen, 4-5/8"x3-3/4" 1		86	–	219
homemade, round, 7" dia. 1		209	–	356
homemade, square, 4-1/2"x4-1/2" . . . 1		140	–	238
Walnuts:				
black, shelled, chopped	1 Tbsp.	50	0	t
Persian or English, in shell	10	322	0	1
Persian or English, shelled, halves	1 cup	651	0	2
Persian or English, shelled, chopped	1 Tbsp.	52	0	t
Waterchestnuts, Chinese (matai) . .	1 oz.	17	0	4
Watercress, fresh:				
chopped	1 cup	24	0	65
whole	1 cup	7	0	18
Watermelon, fresh:				
diced	1 cup	42	0	2
wedge	4" arc	111	0	4
Welsh rarebit	1 cup	415	71	770
Wheat bran (see Flour)				
Wheat cereal (see Cereal)				
Wheat flour (see Flour)				
Wheat germ (see Cereal)				
Wheat parboiled (see Bulgur)				
Whey, fluid	1 cup	59	–	118
Whiskey (see Beverages)				
Whitefish, lake, smoked	4 oz.	176	77	–
White sauce:				
thin	1 cup	303	36	878
medium	1 cup	405	33	948
thick	1 cup	495	30	998

FOOD	AMOUNT	CAL	CHOL (mg.)	SOD (mg.)
Wine (see Beverages)				

Y

Yam, candied (see Potato, sweet)

Yeast:

bakers, compressed, .6 oz. cake . . . 1		15	0	3
bakers, dry, 1/4 oz. pkg. 1		20	0	4
brewer's, debittered . . . . . . 1 Tbsp.		23	0	10
torula . . . . 1 oz.		79	0	4

Yogurt:

from low-fat milk plain . . . . . . 8 oz.		144	14	159
from whole milk . . . . 8 oz.		139	29	105

Youngberries (see Blackberries)

Z

Zucchini (see Squash, summer)
Zwieback (see Crackers)

FOOD	AMOUNT	CAL	CHOL (mg.)	SOD (mg.)

MENU PLANNING LISTS

LOW-CAL BREAKFAST FOODS

Choose from the following low calorie foods to create your own delicious and nutritious breakfast menus. Note that all items contain no more than 150 calories *per serving*. Choose foods from the PROTEIN FOODS section to further enhance your menus.

FOOD	AMOUNT	CAL	CHOL (mg.)	SOD (mg.)
Applesauce:				
canned, unsweetened	1 cup	100	0	5
Apricots:				
canned, unsweetened	1 cup	93	0	2
fresh, halves	1 cup	79	0	2
Banana:				
fresh, 7-3/4" long	1	81	0	1
Blackberries:				
fresh	1 cup	84	0	1
frozen, unsweetened	1 cup	137	0	1
Blueberries:				
fresh	1 cup	90	0	1
frozen, unsweetened	1 cup	91	0	2
Bread:				
cracked wheat	1 sl.	66	t	132
French (2-1/2"x2"x1/2")	1 sl.	44	t	87
raisin	1 sl.	66	t	91
rye	1 sl.	61	t	139
whole wheat	1 sl.	67	t	148
Cantaloupe:				
fresh, 5" dia.	1/2	82	0	33
diced	1 cup	48	0	19
Casaba melon:				
fresh, 5" dia.	1/10	38	0	17
Cereal:				
puffed rice	1 cup	60	0	t
puffed wheat	1 cup	54	0	1

FOOD	AMOUNT	CAL	CHOL (mg.)	SOD (mg.)
shredded wheat	1 biscuit	89	0	t
wheat germ	1 Tbsp.	23	0	t
Cocoa powder, medium fat . . .	1 Tbsp.	14	0	t
Cranberries, fresh, whole	1 cup	44	0	2
Cream substitute, non-dairy . . .	1 Tbsp.	20	0	12
Fruit salad:				
canned, unsweetened	1 cup	86	0	2
Grapefruit:				
canned, unsweetened	1 cup	73	0	10
fresh, 3-9/16" dia.	1/2	40	0	1
fresh, sections	1 cup	82	0	2
Guava, fresh	1 med.	48	0	3
Margarine, regular	1 pat	36	*	49
Milk, skim	1 cup	86	4	126
*Varies, depending on type; can equal zero				
Nectarines, fresh, 2-1/2" dia.	1	88	0	8
Oranges, fresh:				
Navel., 2-7/8" dia.	1	71	0	1
sections	1 cup	88	0	2
Papaya, fresh, cubed	1 cup	55	0	4
Peanut butter, commercial . . .	1 Tbsp.	94	t	97
Pineapple, canned, unsweetened, cuts*	1 cup	96	0	2
Prunes, dried, large	1	22	0	t
Raisins, seedless, whole	1 Tbsp.	26	0	2
Raspberries, fresh:				
black	1 cup	98	0	1
red	1 cup	70	0	1
Strawberries, fresh, whole	1 cup	55	0	1
Tangelo, fresh, 2-3/4" dia.	1	47	0	2
Tangerine, fresh:				
2-1/2" dia.	1	46	0	2
sections	1 cup	90	0	4

FOOD	AMOUNT	CAL	CHOL (mg.)	SOD (mg.)

LOW-CAL LUNCH and DINNER FOODS

Choose from the following low calorie foods to create your own delicious and nutritious lunch and dinner menus. Note that all items contain no more than 150 calories *per serving*. Choose foods from the PROTEIN FOODS section to further enhance your menus.

FOOD	AMOUNT	CAL	CHOL (mg.)	SOD (mg.)
Artichokes:				
French or Globe, cooked	1 bud	16	0	36
Jerusalem, pared, cooked	4 oz.	75	0	2
Asparagus:				
fresh, spears, cooked	1 cup	36	0	2
Bamboo shoots, fresh	1 cup	41	0	1
Beans:				
green or snap, fresh, cooked	1 cup	31	0	5
French style, frozen, cooked	1 cup	34	0	3
sprouts, mung	1 cup	37	0	5
yellow or wax, frozen, cooked	1 cup	36	0	1
Beets, fresh, diced or sliced	1 cup	54	0	73
Beet greens, cooked	1 cup	26	0	110
Boston brown bread:				
canned, 1/2" thick	1 sl.	95	0	113
Bread:				
cracked wheat	1 sl.	66	t	132
French (2-1/2"x2"x1/2")	1 sl.	44	t	87
raisin	1 sl.	66	t	91
rye	1 sl.	61	t	139
whole wheat	1 sl.	67	t	148
Breadsticks, 4-1/2" long	1	38	t	70
Broccoli:				
fresh, stalks	1 med.	47	0	18
frozen, chopped, cooked	1 cup	48	0	28
Brussels sprouts:				
frozen, cooked	1 cup	51	0	22
Cabbage:				
white, wedges, cooked	1 cup	31	0	22

FOOD	AMOUNT	CAL	CHOL (mg.)	SOD (mg.)
Cake, from mix:				
angel food, cubed	1 cu in.	6	0	3
cupcake, uniced, 2-1/2" dia.	1	88	10	113
Carrots:				
fresh, 7" long	1	30	0	34
fresh, sliced, cooked	1 cup	48	0	51
Cauliflower:				
fresh, whole buds	1 cup	27	0	13
frozen, cooked	1 cup	32	0	18
Celery, fresh, 8" long	1 stalk	7	0	50
Chard, Swiss, fresh, cooked	1 cup	26	0	125
Cheese straws, 5" long	1	27	2	43
Cherries, sour, fresh:				
whole (pitted)	1 cup	90	0	3
Collards:				
fresh, cooked	1 cup	63	0	40
frozen, chopped, cooked	1 cup	51	0	27
Cookies:				
butter thins, 2" dia.	1	23	3	21
graham crackers, plain	2" sq.	28	t	48
Corn, fresh:				
on the cob, cooked	5" ear	70	0	t
Crackers:				
butter, round, 1-7/8" dia.	1	15	t	36
rye wafers, 3-1/2"x1-7/8"	1	22	0	57
soda, 1-7/8" sq.	1	12	0	31
soda, biscuit, 2-3/8"x2-1/8"	1	22	0	55
wheat thins	4	55	t	23
zwieback, 3-1/2"x1-1/2"	1	30	t	18
Cress, garden, cooked	1 cup	31	0	11
Cucumber, peeled, sliced	1 cup	20	0	8
Dandelion greens, cooked	1 cup	35	0	46
Endive, fresh, chopped	1 cup	10	0	7
Fruit cocktail:				
canned, unsweetened	1 cup	91	0	12

FOOD	AMOUNT	CAL	CHOL (mg.)	SOD (mg.)
Fruit salad:				
canned, unsweetened	1 cup	86	0	2
Kale:				
fresh, cooked	1 cup	43	0	47
frozen, cooked	1 cup	40	0	27
Kohlrabi, fresh:				
diced, cooked	1 cup	40	0	10
Lettuce, raw:				
iceberg, wedge	1/4 head	18	0	12
romaine, chopped	1 cup	10	0	5
Mushrooms, fresh:				
chopped or sliced	1 cup	20	0	10
Mustard greens:				
fresh, cooked	1 cup	32	0	25
frozen, chopped, cooked	1 cup	30	0	15
Okra:				
fresh, sliced, cooked	1 cup	46	0	3
frozen, sliced, cooked	1 cup	70	0	4
Onions:				
green, tops only, chopped (scallions)	1 Tbsp.	2	0	t
mature, whole or sliced, cooked	1 cup	61	0	15
Parsley, fresh, whole sprigs	10 .	4	0	5
Parsnips:				
cooked, whole, 6" long	1	23	0	3
Peaches:				
canned, unsweetened	1 cup	76	0	5
fresh, 2-1/2" dia.	1	38	0	1
Peanut butter, commercial . . .	1 Tbsp.	94	t	97
Pears:				
canned, unsweetened	1 cup	78	0	2
fresh, Bartlett, 2-1/2" dia.	1	100	0	3
fresh, Bosc, 2-1/2" dia.	1	86	0	3
Peppers, sweet:				
green, 3" dia.	1 ring	2	0	1

FOOD	AMOUNT	CAL	CHOL (mg.)	SOD (mg.)
green, sliced	1 cup	18	0	10
red, 3" dia.	1 ring	3	0	t
Pickles, sweet:				
chopped	1 Tbsp.	15	0	69
gherkin, midget	1	9	0	48
mustard (Chow-chow)	1 Tbsp.	18	0	81
Pineapple:				
canned, unsweetened, cuts*	1 cup	96	0	2
fresh, sliced, 3-1/2" dia.	1	44	0	1
chunk, tidbit, crushed				
Plums, fresh:				
Damson, 1" dia.	10	66	0	2
Japanese, diced	1 cup	79	0	2
prune-type, 1-1/2" dia.	1	21	0	t
Raisins, seedless, whole	1 Tbsp.	26	0	2
Rhubarb, fresh, diced	1 cup	20	0	2
Rutabagas:				
fresh, cooked, mashed	1 cup	84	0	10
Salad dressings, commercial:				
French, low-calorie	1 Tbsp.	15	0	126
Italian, low-calorie	1 Tbsp.	8	0	t
Russian, low-calorie	1 Tbsp.	23	1	26
Salad dressing (mayonnaise-type)	1 Tbsp.	65	4	88
Salad dressing, low-calorie	1 Tbsp.	22	t	19
Thousand Island, low-calorie	1 Tbsp.	27	2	105
Soybean				
curd (tofu), 2-1/2"x2-3/4"	1 piece	86	0	8
sprouts	1 cup	48	0	3
Spinach:				
fresh, chopped	1 cup	14	0	39
frozen, leaf, cooked	1 cup	46	0	93
Squash, summer:				
fresh, cooked, sliced	1 cup	29	0	2
Squash, winter, fresh:				
acorn, baked, 4" dia.	1/2	86	0	2

FOOD	AMOUNT	CAL	CHOL (mg.)	SOD (mg.)
butternut, boiled, mashed . . .	1 cup	100	0	2
hubbard, boiled, diced	1 cup	71	0	2
Tomatoes:				
fresh, 2-3/5" dia.	1	27	0	4
fresh, cooked	1 cup	63	0	10
Turnip, cooked, mashed	1 cup	53	0	78
Turnip greens:				
frozen, chopped, cooked	1 cup	38	0	28
Waterchestnuts, Chinese	1 oz.	17	0	4
Watercress, fresh, chopped	1 cup	24	0	65
Watermelon, fresh, diced	1 cup	42	0	2

LOW-CAL SNACKS

Choose from the following low calorie foods to create your own delicious and nutritious snacks. Note that all items contain no more than 150 calories *per serving*. Choose foods from the PROTEIN FOODS section to further enhance your snacks.

FOOD	AMOUNT	CAL	CHOL (mg.)	SOD (mg.)
Apples, fresh, whole, 3" dia.	1	96	0	2
Applesauce:				
canned, unsweetened	1 cup	100	0	5
Apricots, fresh, whole	3	55	0	1
Banana, fresh, 7-3/4" long	1	81	0	1
Blackberries, fresh	1 cup	84	0	1
Blueberries, fresh	1 cup	90	0	1
Breadsticks, 4-1/2" long	1	38	t	70
Cake, from mix:				
angel food, cubed	1 cu. in.	6	0	3
Celery, fresh, 8" long	1 stalk	7	0	50
Cherries, sour, fresh,				
whole (pitted)	1 cup	90	0	3
Crackers:				
butter, round, 1-7/8" dia.	1	15	t	36
rye wafers, 3-1/2"x1-7/8"	1	22	0	57
soda, 1-7/8" sq.	1	12	0	31

FOOD	AMOUNT	CAL	CHOL (mg.)	SOD (mg.)
soda, biscuit, 2-3/8"x2-1/8" 1		22	0	55
wheat thins 4		55	t	23
zwieback, 3-1/2"x1-1/2" 1		30	t	18
Fig:				
dried 1		55	0	7
fresh, 2-1/4" dia. 1		40	0	1
Gooseberries, fresh	1 cup	59	0	2
Granadilla (Passion fruit), fresh 1		16	0	5
Grapefruit, fresh, 3-9/16" dia.	1/2	40	0	1
Grapes, fresh, American-type . . .	1 cup	70	0	3
Guava, fresh	1 med.	48	0	3
Kumquat, fresh	1 sm.	15	0	5
Loganberries, fresh	1 cup	89	0	1
Lychees, fresh 10		58	0	3
Margarine, regular . . . . 1 pat		36	*	49
*varies, depending on type; can equal zero				
Nectarines, fresh, 2-1/2" dia. 1		88	0	8
Oranges, fresh, Navel, 2-7/8" dia. 1		71	0	1
Papaya, fresh, cubed	1 cup	55	0	4
Peaches, fresh:				
2-1/2" dia. 1		38	0	1
diced	1 cup	70	0	2
Peanut butter, commercial . . .	1 Tbsp.	94	t	97
Peanuts, roasted, shell, jumbo 10		105	0	1
Pears, fresh:				
Bartlett, 2-1/2" dia. 1		100	0	3
Bosc, 2-1/2" dia. 1		86	0	3
Peppers, sweet:				
green, 3" dia.	1 ring	2	0	1
red, 3" dia.	1 ring	3	0	1
Pickles, sweet:				
chopped	1 Tbsp.	15	0	69
gherkin midget 1		9	0	48
mustard				
(Chow-chow)	1 Tbsp.	18	0	81

FOOD	AMOUNT	CAL	CHOL (mg.)	SOD (mg.)
Pineapple:				
canned, unsweetened cuts**	1 cup	96	0	2
fresh, sliced, 3-1/2" dia.	1	44	0	1
**chunks, crushed, tidbits*				
Plums, fresh:				
Damson, 1" dia.	10	66	0	2
Japanese, 2-1/8" dia.	1	32	0	1
prune-type, 1-1/2" dia.	1	21	0	t
Pomegranate, fresh, 3-3/8" dia.	1	97	0	5
Popcorn, plain	1 cup	23	0	t
Prunes, dried, large	1	22	0	t
Radishes, fresh, large	10	14	0	15
Raisins, seedless, whole	1 Tbsp.	2.6	0	2
Raspberries, fresh:				
black	1 cup	98	0	1
red	1 cup	70	0	1
Rusk, 3-3/8" dia.	1	38	t	22
Strawberries, fresh, whole	1 cup	55	0	1
Tangelo, fresh, 2-3/4" dia.	1	47	0	2
Tangerine, fresh, 2-1/2" dia.	1	46	0	2

LOW-CAL BEVERAGES

Choose from the following low-calorie beverages for meals or snacks. Note that all items contain no more than 120 calories *per serving*.

FOOD	AMOUNT	CAL	CHOL (mg.)	SOD (mg.)
Apple juice, canned or bottled	1 cup	117	0	2
Beverages, alcoholic:				
beer, "light"	12 oz.	96	0	–
wine, table (12% alcohol)	3-1/2 oz.	87	0	5
Beverages, carbonated:				
club soda, unsweetened	12 oz.	0	0	39
tonic water	12 oz.	113	0	19
Blackberry juice, canned,				
unsweetened	1 cup	91	0	2

FOOD	AMOUNT	CAL	CHOL (mg.)	SOD (mg.)
Cocoa:				
beverage powder	1 oz.	98	0	76
medium-fat powder	1 Tbsp.	14	0	t
Coffee, prepared, plain	1 cup	2	0	2
Grapefruit juice:				
canned, unsweetened	1 cup	101	0	2
fresh	1 cup	96	0	2
Grapefruit-orange juice, canned unsweetened	1 cup	106	0	2
Lemonade, frozen, sweetened	1 cup	107	0	1
Limeade, frozen, sweetened	1 cup	102	0	t
Milk:				
low-fat, 2%	1 cup	121	18	122
skim	1 cup	86	4	126
Orange juice:				
fresh	1 cup	112	0	2
frozen, unsweetened	1 cup	114	0	2
Tangelo juice, fresh	1 cup	101	0	2
Tangerine juice:				
canned, unsweetened	1 cup	106	0	2
fresh	1 cup	106	0	2

BREAKFAST *PROTEIN* FOODS

Choose from the following low calorie protein foods to enhance your breakfasts. Note that all items contain no more than *200 calories per serving*. In moderate amounts, these nutritious foods provide ample protein without contributing excessive amounts of calories.

FOOD	AMOUNT	CAL	CHOL (mg.)	SOD (mg.)
Cottage cheese, uncreamed	1 cup	123	10	19
Milk:				
low fat, 2%	1 cup	121	18	122
skim	1 cup	86	4	126
Sardines, Atlantic, canned, 3" long	1	24	25	99
Sausage, pork, fresh, cooked	1 link	62	10	125
Yogurt, from lowfat milk, plain	8 oz.	144	14	159

FOOD	AMOUNT	CAL	CHOL (mg.)	SOD (mg.)

LUNCH and DINNER *PROTEIN* FOODS

Choose from the following low calorie protein foods to enhance your lunches and dinners. Note that all items contain no more than *200 calories per serving*. In moderate amounts, these nutritious foods provide ample protein without contributing excessive amounts of calories.

FOOD	AMOUNT	CAL	CHOL (mg.)	SOD (mg.)
Beef, lean, trimmed, cooked:				
chuck, roast or steak	3 oz.	164	77	45
flank steak (London broil)	3 oz.	167	77	45
ground, 10% fat	3 oz.	186	77	57
round steak	3 oz.	161	77	65
rump roast	3 oz.	177	77	61
sirloin, double-bone	3 oz.	184	77	64
sirloin wedge- and round-bone	3 oz.	176	77	67
Bluefish, fresh, baked with margarine	4 oz.	185	63	118
Cheese:				
Brie	1 oz.	95	28	178
Brick	1 oz.	105	27	159
Cheddar, domestic	1 oz.	114	30	176
Colby	1 oz.	112	27	171
Cottage, uncreamed	1 cup	123	10	19
Mozzarella, part-skim	1 oz.	72	16	132
Muenster	1 oz.	104	27	178
Neufchatel	1 oz.	74	22	113
Parmesan, grated	1 Tbsp.	23	4	93
Swiss, domestic	1 oz.	107	26	74
Chicken:				
broiler	3 oz.	116	69	56
roaster	3 oz.	156	69	75
Cod, fresh, broiled with margarine	4 oz.	192	65	124
Goose, domesticated, cooked	3 oz.	198	36	105
Haddock, fresh, oven-fried	4 oz.	188	77	200
Halibut, fresh, broiled with margarine	4 oz.	192	77	152

FOOD	AMOUNT	CAL	CHOL (mg.)	SOD (mg.)
Ham:				
boiled . . . . 1 oz.		66	70	49
deviled, canned . . . . 1 Tbsp.		46	15	122
fresh . . . . 3 oz.		184	80	62
fresh shoulder pork (Picnic) . . . 3 oz.		180	75	43
Rockfish, fresh, cooked . . . . . . 4 oz.		120	65	96
Sardines, Atlantic, canned, 3" long . . . 1		24	25	99
Smelt, fresh, cooked . . . . 4 oz.		100	77	30
Sole, fresh, cooked . . . . 4 oz.		90	77	89
Swordfish, fresh, broiled				
with margarine . . . . 4 oz.		184	77	—
Tongue, beef, cooked . . . . . . 2 oz.		138	66	35
Tuna:				
canned in water . . . . 4 oz.		144	72	46
fresh, cooked . . . . 3 oz.		105	60	46
Turkey, cooked, light meat . . . . 3 oz.		150	65	70

PROTEIN SNACKS

Choose from the following low calorie protein foods to enhance your snacks. Note that all items contain no more than *200 calories per serving*. In moderate amounts, these nutritious foods provide ample protein without contributing excessive amounts of calories.

FOOD	AMOUNT	CAL	CHOL (mg.)	SOD (mg.)
Almonds, dried, shelled,				
chopped . . . . 1 Tbsp.		48	0	t
Brazil nuts, shelled, large 6		185	0	t
Cheese (see Lunch and Dinner Selections above)				
Cheese straws, 5" long 1		27	2	43
Chestnuts, in shell 10		141	0	4
Filberts 10		87	0	t
Ham, boiled . . . . 1 oz.		66	70	49
Ice milk, plain, 5% fat . . . . . . 1 cup		184	18	105
Pecans, shelled, chopped . . . . 1 Tbsp.		52	0	t
Sardines, Atlantic, canned, 3" long . . . 1		24	25	99
Walnuts, shelled, chopped . . . . 1 Tbsp.		52	0	t
Yogurt, from lowfat milk, plain . . . 8 oz.		144	14	159

FOOD	AMOUNT	CAL	CHOL (mg.)	SOD (mg.)

CHOLESTEROL-REDUCING FOODS

Choose from the following low calorie foods *to help reduce cholesterol* while you lose weight. Note that all items contain no more than *200 calories per serving*. Each item is a rich source of dietary factors that can help bring your cholesterol down—without interfering with your weight control program!

OMEGA-3
CHOLESTEROL-REDUCING FOODS

FOOD	AMOUNT	CAL	CHOL (mg.)	SOD (mg.)
anchovies	10	70	22	230
bluefish	3.5 oz	117	74	55
clams	1/2 cup	79	50	96
crab	1/2 cup	58	58	575
cod	3.5 oz	78	60	70
flounder	3.5 oz	79	50	78
haddock	3.5 oz	79	60	61
herring, in oil	3.5 oz	169	87	4,985
in tomato sauce	2	194	86	82
lobster, cooked	3.5 oz	95	85	210
mackerel, canned	3.5 oz	180	94	—
mussels (meat only)	3.5 oz	95	50	289
oysters	1/2 cup	79	60	88
salmon, canned (pink)	3-3/8 oz	155	39	425
fresh	3.5 oz	182	33	50
sardines, in oil	3.5 oz	200	120	823
in tomato sauce	3.5 oz	197	110	400
scallops	3.5 oz	194	41	120
shrimp, canned	1/2 cup	75	96	89
raw	3.5 oz	91	150	140
swordfish	3.5 oz	118	55	54
trout, lake	3.5 oz	168	55	81

FOOD	AMOUNT	CAL	CHOL (mg.)	SOD (mg.)
tuna, in oil	3.5 oz	197	65	800
in water (salt-free)	3.5 oz	127	63	41

MONOUNSATURATED
CHOLESTEROL-REDUCING FOODS

FOOD	AMOUNT	CAL	CHOL	SOD
almonds	1 oz	170	0	1
avocado, California	1/2	185	0	4
Florida	1/2	196	0	6
cashews	1 oz	159	0	4
filberts (hazelnuts)	1 oz	180	0	1
olive oil	1 tsp	30	0	0
olives, black, Greek-style	5 lg	45	0	434
peanut oil	1 tsp	30	0	0
peanuts	1 oz	166	0	119
pecans	1 oz	195	0	t

SOLUBLE FIBER
CHOLESTEROL-REDUCING FOODS

FOOD	AMOUNT	CAL	CHOL	SOD
Dried Beans and Peas:				
black-eyed peas, cooked	1/2 cup	89	0	1
garbanzos (chickpeas)	1/4 cup	155	0	13
kidney beans, cooked	1/2 cup	109	0	3
lentils, cooked	1/2 cup	106	0	—
lima beans, cooked	1/2 cup	131	0	2
navy beans, cooked	1/2 cup	112	0	6
canned (no pork)	1/2 cup	153	0	431
soybeans, cooked	1/2 cup	117	0	2
split peas, cooked	1/2 cup	115	0	13
tofu	4 oz	82	0	—
Oat Products:				
oat bran, uncooked	1 oz	110	0	0
oatmeal, cooked	1 cup	132	0	523
oat muffins (made with egg whites)	1 av	120	0	175

GLOSSARY

ANGINA — chest pain from lack of oxygen, due to blockage of coronary arteries.

ARTERIOSCLEROSIS — "hardening of the arteries;" walls of arteries become thick, hard, and inflexible, leading to elevated blood pressure.

ATHEROSCLEROSIS — a form of arteriosclerosis; inner walls of arteries roughen and thicken as they develop deposits of cholesterol and other fatty materials, eventually slowing or halting blood flow.

BLOOD PRESSURE — force exerted by the heart as it pumps blood out through the arteries to all areas of the body.

CALCIUM — an essential mineral responsible for bone strength, proper heartbeat and nervous system function.

CARDIOVASCULAR DISEASE — disease of the arteries including heart attack (arteries to the heart), circulatory disorders (arteries to the extremities), and stroke (arteries to the brain).

CHOLESTEROL — a waxy, fat-like substance produced by the liver and supplied by diet; found only in animal foods (notably egg yolk and organ meats), and as an element of atherosclerotic deposits.

CLAUDICATION — numbness in the legs associated with atherosclerosis.

CONGESTIVE HEART FAILURE — heart weakening due to fluid accumulation in tissues.

"CORONARY" — myocardial infarction or heart attack.

CORONARY ARTERIES — vessels carrying blood to the heart; heart attack results when these arteries are blocked by clots or fatty acids.

DIURETIC — medication to reduce edema; "water pill."

EDEMA — abnormal accumulation of fluid in tissues (swelling); treatment includes diuretic medication and low sodium diet.

ESSENTIAL FATTY ACIDS — portion of fat required in small amounts in the diet (1-2% of total caloric intake) to prevent deficiency.

FIBER — indigestible plant material which aids digestion process and plays a preventive role in certain chronic diseases, including heart disease.

HDL — "high density lipoprotein;" a blood protein that transports fats and cleans cholesterol from the bloodstream.

HEART ATTACK — myocardial infarction or "coronary."

HYDROGENATION — process for solidifying fats by adding hydrogen; used to lengthen shelf life of such foods as shortening, margarine, and peanut butter.

HYPERLIPIDEMIA — condition of excessive blood levels of fat-like substances, including cholesterol and triglycerides.

HYPERTENSION — high blood pressure; force in arteries is above normal due to disease (secondary hypertension) or from unknown causes (essential hypertension); treatment includes diet, drugs, and/or stress reduction techniques.

ISCHEMIA — local lack of blood supply, usually due to narrowed arteries.

LECITHIN — a kind of fat found in soybeans, corn, and eggs, and added as an emulsifier to many processed foods; assists fat transport in the blood, but no scientific evidence exists to support claims for lecithin as a cholesterol-lowering aid.

LDL — "low density lipoprotein;" a blood protein that carries fats and cholesterol from the liver to other tissues; an elevated level is *directly* correlated with increased risk of heart disease.

LIPIDS — fats or fat-like substances including cholesterol, triglycerides, and dietary fats.

LIPOPROTEINS — type of protein in blood which transports fats; used to determine blood fat levels for discovering hyperlipidemias.

MAGNESIUM — an essential mineral found in nuts, dried beans and peas, whole grains, green leafy vegetables, and seafood; deficiency may contribute to high blood pressure and heart failure.

MINERALS — naturally occurring elements; there are seventeen currently recognized as essential for growth and optimal health, including calcium, magnesium, potassium, and sodium.

MONOUNSATURATED FATS — partially unsaturated fats found in olives, olive and peanut oils, nuts, and avocado; substitute for saturated fats to help lower blood cholesterol levels.

MYOCARDIAL INFARCTION — heart attack or "coronary;" blockage of blood to the heart through one or more coronary artery results in lack of oxygen to parts of the heart muscle (myocardium), causing these parts to die.

NIACIN — a B-vitamin found in meats, poultry, fish, dried beans and peas, and peanut butter; supplements taken in large doses (as niacin, nicotinic acid, or niacinamide) can cause harmful side effects, including flushing and itching, irregular heartbeat, and liver damage.

OMEGA-3 FATTY ACIDS — polyunsaturated fatty acids found in cold water fish and shellfish; adequate intakes can help to reduce blood cholesterol levels and blood pressure, and prevent blood clotting and heart disease.

POLYUNSATURATED FATS — fats that are usually liquid at room temperature including corn, cottonseed, safflower, sesame, soybean, and sunflower oils; substitute for saturated fats to help lower blood cholesterol levels.

POTASSIUM — an essential mineral that helps to maintain proper heartbeat.

SATURATED FATS — fats that are usually solid at room temperature; found primarily in animal foods (butter, cheese, cream, lard, meats, and whole milk) and in coconut oil, cocoa butter, palm oil, and hydrogenated fats and oils. Limiting intake can help to lower blood cholesterol levels.

SODIUM — an essential mineral found in table salt (sodium chloride) and most foods, notably processed convenience and fast foods.

TRIGLYCERIDE — type of lipid formed in the body from sugar and alcohol.

VITAMIN E — an essential mineral found in vegetable oils, olive and peanut oils, wheat germ and whole grains, dried beans and peas, nuts, and olives; supplements taken in large doses can cause unpleasant side effects.

APPENDIX A

THE SURGEON GENERAL'S DIETARY RECOMMENDATIONS

The 1988 report issued by the U.S. Surgeon General addresses the impact of the American diet on the country's health. For the majority of citizens, the major problem is overeating with nutritional imbalances. Based on an extensive review of the most current scientific evidence, the guidelines recommended by this important report include the following issues:

FATS AND CHOLESTEROL — Reduce consumption of fat (especially saturated fat) and cholesterol.

ENERGY AND WEIGHT CONTROL — Achieve and maintain a desirable body weight. Increase energy expenditure through regular and sustained physical activity.

COMPLEX CARBOHYDRATES AND FIBER — Increase consumption of whole grain foods and cereal products, vegetables (including dried beans and peas), and fruits.

SODIUM — Reduce intake of sodium by choosing foods relatively low in sodium and limiting the amount of salt added in food preparation and at the table.

ALCOHOL — To reduce the risk of chronic disease, take alcohol only in moderation (no more than two drinks a day), if at all. Avoid drinking any alcohol before or while driving, operating machinery, taking medications, or engaging in any other activity requiring judgement. Avoid drinking while pregnant.

APPENDIX B

PERSONAL WEIGHT CHART

Record your weight once a week in the chart on this page. Then, plot your weight on the graph so that you can visualize your progress more easily.

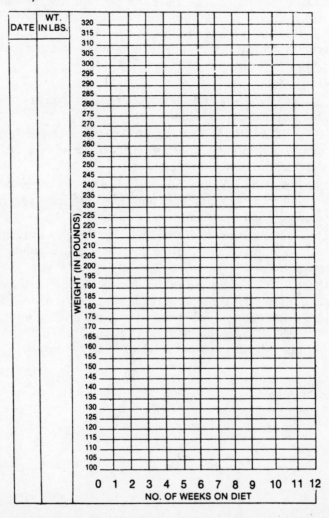

APPENDIX C

DESIRED WEIGHT CHART

Normal weights for Americans ages 25-59, as determined by the Metropolitan Life Insurance Co., base on small, medium or large frames.

HGT.	WEIGHTS FOR MEN			WEIGHTS FOR WOMEN		
	Small	Medium	Large	Small	Medium	Large
4-10				102-111	109-121	118-131
4-11				103-113	111-123	120-134
5-0				104-115	113-126	122-137
5-1				106-118	115-129	125-140
5-2	128-134	131-141	138-150	108-121	118-132	128-143
5-3	130-136	133-143	140-153	111-124	121-135	131-147
5-4	132-138	135-145	142-156	114-127	124-138	134-151
5-5	134-140	137-148	144-160	117-130	127-141	137-155
5-6	136-142	139-151	146-164	120-133	130-144	140-159
5-7	138-145	142-154	149-168	123-136	133-147	143-163
5-8	140-148	145-157	152-172	126-139	136-150	146-167
5-9	142-151	148-160	155-176	129-142	139-153	149-170
5-10	144-154	151-163	158-180	132-145	142-156	152-173
5-11	146-157	154-166	161-184	135-148	145-159	155-176
6-0	149-160	157-170	164-188	138-151	148-162	158-179
6-1	152-164	160-174	168-192			
6-2	155-168	164-178	172-197			
6-3	158-172	167-182	176-202			
6-4	162-176	171-187	181-207			

Height is in feet and inches with shoes with 1-inch heels. Weight is in pounds, with indoor clothing weighing 5 pounds for men and 3 pounds for women. For girls between 18 and 25, subtract 1 pound for each year under 25.

APPENDIX D

MAXIMUM CALORIES PER DAY

WOMEN	Age 18-35	Age 35-55	Age 55-75
To Maintain This Weight	Daily Intake of Calories	Daily Intake of Calories	Daily Intake of Calories
Pounds			
100	1700	1500	1300
110	1850	1650	1400
120	2000	1750	1550
130	2125	1925	1625
145	2300	2050	1800
155	2500	2250	2000

MEN	Age 18-35	Age 35-55	Age 55-75
To Maintain This Weight	Daily Intake of Calories	Daily Intake of Calories	Daily Intake of Calories
Pounds			
110	2200	1950	1700
120	2400	2150	1900
130	2525	2275	2025
140	2700	2400	2250
155	2800	2600	2400
165	3100	2800	2650
175	3250	3000	2850
185	3400	3200	3000

APPENDIX E

CONVERSION TABLES

Common Measurements Use the table below to assist you in converting given quantites of foods into the desired equivalents.

```
        5 milliliters = 1 teaspoon
        3 teaspoons = 1 tablespoon
    16 tablespoons = 1 cup = 8 fluid ounces
             2 cups = 1 pint = 16 fluid ounces
            2 pints = 1 quart = 32 fluid ounces
          4 quarts = 1 gallon = 128 fluid ounces
     28.35 grams = 1 ounce = 2 fluid tablespoons
        16 ounces = 1 pound = 453.6 grams
          8 quarts = 1 peck
          4 pecks = 1 bushel
```

US to Metric Measurements The U.S. Department of Agriculture uses the following rounded figures for converting quantities of foods, energy values, and temperatures into metric system equivalents.

U.S. SYSTEM	Metric System Equivalent
	Length:
1 inch	2.54 centimeters,
	25.4 millimeters
	Volume:
1 cubic inch	16.39 cubic centimeters
1 teaspoon	5 milliliters
1 tablespoon	15 milliliters
1 fluid ounce	30 milliliters
1 cup	240 milliliters
1 pint	475 milliliters
1 quart	950 milliliters
1 gallon	3.8 liters
	Energy:
1 kilocalorie	4.184 kiloJoules
	Temperature:
1° Fahrenheit (F)	5/9° Celsius (C)